ELECTRONIC RESUMES THAT GET JOBS

Dedicated to Saundra and Travis,
with love and gratitude.

ACKNOWLEDGMENTS

My thanks go out to a number of people who helped to bring this book into print. Linda Bernbach, my editor at Arco Publishing, has been consistently encouraging and supportive. Janet Stumper and Maia Coven-Reim literally turned my words into a book with their graphic design skills. Art Ungar, of Success Strategies in Lawrenceville, New Jersey, and Marilyn Silverman, of Word Center Printing in Hamilton Square, New Jersey, generously shared their resources. David Bernstein graciously commented on the draft version. Thanks also go to the readers of the seventh and eighth editions of *Resumes That Get Jobs* for their reactions and suggestions.

Finally, and most importantly, I am indebted to Saundra Young and Travis Potter for their love, patience, and understanding.

Ray Potter
Hopewell, New Jersey

Cartoons by Eli Stein used by permission of the artist.

ELECTRONIC RESUMES THAT GET JOBS

RAY POTTER

Macmillan General Reference
A Simon & Schuster Macmillan Company
1633 Broadway
New York, NY 10019-6785

An Arco Book

ARCO, MACMILLAN and colophons are registered
trademarks of Simon & Schuster Inc.

Maufactured in the United States of America

10 9 8 7 6 5 4 3 2 1

ISBN 0-02-861045-8

PREFACE

Maybe you have heard it said that computers have completely changed the way people look for work today. Every time you browse through a magazine or newspaper these days, you're likely to see phrases like "the electronic revolution," "the information superhighway," and "on-line databases." If you're like most people who are trying to write or update a resume, you're wondering exactly how all of this computerization affects you. What does it all mean for you? How can you develop a resume that competes in this new world of computerized job searching? What should a resume look like these days? How can you write one yourself? These are exactly the kinds of questions that this book can answer.

It is true that computerization has changed many aspects of the job search. However, it's still true that you need a resume if you're looking for a job. In fact, resumes are required in more occupational fields than ever before. And to be effective in this new electronic world—to make a positive impact on a potential employer—a resume has to be written for computers as well as for people. Of course resumes are still read by people but, increasingly, resumes are being "read" by computers too. That means that your resume now has to work twice as hard. It has to make its impact not just on the person who might call you in for an interview, but on the computer that is used by the person who makes that call.

This book can teach you how to create a resume that gets attention from computers as well as from the employers who use them. In a clear, straightforward way, you will learn exactly how computers are being used in the hiring process and you will learn how you can take advantage of your new knowledge to design an up-to-the-minute resume. If you follow the simple process that is outlined in these pages, you will develop a resume that will stand out from the crowd—a resume that will be as effective with computerized search systems as it is with the real people who are searching for new employees.

This book isn't intended only for people who work in high-tech job fields or just for people who work with computers every day. It's for everyone who wants to write a resume. If you're wondering if this is the book for you, the answer is "YES"! It doesn't assume that you already know how to write a resume or how to conduct a job search in today's computerized environment (although it can still help you if you do). Instead, it is filled with simple, easy-to-understand explanations, advice, tips, suggestions, and worksheets. Everything you need to create your own best resume is right here in the pages ahead.

Developing a resume, even in the computer age, isn't as difficult as some people (and some books) would lead you to believe. The experience doesn't have to be painful or tedious and the process doesn't have to be shrouded in myth or mystery. This is a book that takes the mystery out of writing a resume and replaces it with mastery! If you want to create a resume that presents the best picture of you to a possible employer (and who doesn't?), this is the book for you.

In fact, this is really two books in one. In the first sections you will learn how computerization has affected the job search process and you will see how resumes are being electronically stored, retrieved, and "read" by computers. You will discover a wealth of new resources for job seekers, including on-line databanks filled with job openings. And you will learn how to step onto the Internet and use its mind-boggling array of offerings to help you find a job. In the second part of the book, you will be taken step-by-step through the process of creating your own best resume. The process is based on the method outlined in the latest edition of one of the best-selling resume preparation guidebooks of all time: *Resumes That Get Jobs*. As more than a million people can attest, this is an approach that works!

As you develop your resume, you will learn a few things about the job market today, including where your resume really goes after you put it into the mail or drop it off at an office. You will be able to apply what you learn in order to craft a resume that can compete against all of the other resumes that end up on an employer's desk along with yours. When you have finished writing your resume, you can be confident that it is ready for competition. It will be ready to present you—with all of your skills, qualifications, experiences, and accomplishments—to the world. This is a big job for a resume, but your resume will be up to the challenge.

Let's get started!

"Glad to meet you Mr. Nagle. I'm awfully sorry, but I seem to have misplaced your resume."

TABLE OF CONTENTS

INTRODUCTION

YOUR RESUME IN THE ELECTRONIC AGE

Computerization has affected so many areas of contemporary life that it's no surprise that computers have had an impact on the ways in which job seekers look for work today. Just as computers are being put to work in the hiring departments of companies large and small, savvy job seekers can put computers to work in their own job searches. However, to take advantage of the opportunities afforded by computerization, you have to know two things: how computers are being used by employers and how you can utilize them when you're looking for a new job.

This book will introduce you to the ways in which electronic information about prospective employees is being solicited, stored, and retrieved by employers and then it will show you how you can make yourself into a more desirable, more "hirable" job applicant. The education you receive here will give you an advantage in today's job market. And let's face it: you need every advantage you can get.

The job market is a very competitive place these days. It's common to hear reports from employers who regularly receive several hundred applications for every job they advertise. And contrary to what you might have assumed, it's not necessarily the best-

qualified candidates who end up getting the jobs. Often the most successful job seekers are those who have the best knowledge of the hiring process. They understand what happens to their resumes after they put them into the mail. They know how to write resumes that can be "read" by computers as well as by humans. They are comfortable with the new technologies and know how put them to work.

Successful job seekers—those who actually land jobs—have also learned to "think like an employer." They know how to read ads and job descriptions to figure out exactly what employers want. In response, they have learned how to write resumes and cover letters that make them stand out from a crowd of applicants. They look interesting on paper and on-line—interesting enough that employers want to meet them. They are the candidates who are invited in for interviews. They are the candidates who get jobs.

This book can make you a better job seeker. It can help you stand out from the crowd. There are two ways that it accomplishes this task.

First, it introduces you to the ways in which information that was once kept on paper, in filing cabinets, is now stored on computers. It shows you how to "think like a computer," so that you can prepare a resume that is ready for the electronic treatment it will receive in the new world of work. And it shows you how to use easily available computerized resources to enhance your job search. Second, it teaches you how to write your own best resume—one that utilizes everything that you have learned in the first section of this book.

There are three specific ways in which computers are playing an increasingly important role in today's hiring process:

1) **Applicant Tracking Systems.** These are the computer software packages now in use by companies of all sizes to electronically file and retrieve resumes.

2) **Job Databanks.** There are now large-scale databases that are filled with listings of available jobs—and available job seekers. Maintained by many different kinds of organizations, these can be a tremendous resource for anyone who is looking for a new job.

3) **The Internet.** The Internet, and the on-line databases known collectively as "the information superhighway," have already had a major impact on how people learn about and apply for jobs—and they will have an even greater impact in the future.

Not only does each of these areas get its own chapter in this book, but each chapter is filled with tips and

suggestions on making these new systems work on your behalf. In the pages that follow you will learn how these new systems function and how you can create resumes that increase your chances of being noticed within these systems. Since every one of these information systems is capable of storing the resumes of thousands of job candidates, getting noticed is exactly the result you want.

After you have learned the new ways that your resume can be put to work in the electronic age, you will be guided through a step-by-step process of creating your own best resume. Everything you need is right here in this book. There are clear instructions, easy-to-use worksheets, and lots of sample resumes.

As you work your way through this book, you will be actually writing your resume. By the time you finish the book, you should have a new resume (or several new resumes) designed to work in all computerized systems—and in systems that still use paper and filing cabinets too!

Whether you are writing your first resume or your fiftieth, looking for an entry-level job or an executive position, reentering the workforce or ready to move up, changing careers or continuing on your job path, this book can help you. There's a lot to learn, but there's a big reward as well: the prospect of a new job! Take a deep breath, turn the page, and plunge in. You'll be glad you did.

CHAPTER 1

RESUMES AND TRACKING SYSTEMS

WHAT HAPPENS TO YOUR RESUME ANYWAY?

Do you ever wonder what happens to your resume after you send it off to a potential employer? Do you think about how it is filed—and how it is retrieved? Have you ever received a letter that informs you that "your resume is being kept on file"? Did that letter make you speculate about how it would be found at some point in the future? Well, you're not alone. Most job applicants have had questions like these at one time or another.

In the days Before Computers ("B.C."), resumes were filed in filing cabinets. Probably they were kept in the Personnel Department (however large or small it was), and they sat there untouched until there was a job opening. When there was a position available, a department manager somewhere in the company made a phone call or sent a requisition form to Personnel describing the position and the qualifications of the kind of person who could fill it.

Then it was someone's job to "see who's in the files." This person, who might have had a title like "Personnel Assistant" or "Recruiter," would go to the filing cabinets and take a look inside. He or she would select the resumes of people who looked like they met the specifications that the manager had set, would make a photocopy of the resumes, and would send them off to the manager who had requested them.

Actually, the process wasn't as efficient as it might sound from the description above. The reason that it wasn't more efficient is simple. The resumes weren't organized very well and the person who looked through them had to spend a lot of time trying to find the resumes that matched the latest requisition. No matter how hard companies tried to streamline the process, it was still cumbersome. And the more resumes the company had on file, the more difficult it was to find specific ones when they were needed.

Usually the best results that the Personnel Assistant could produce came from looking into the files of resumes that had been collected the last time that an identical (or at least similar) position had been available. However, that could have been years ago and perhaps only a handful of the candidates for that old position would still be interested in the new one.

COMPUTERS ARE TODAY'S FILING CABINETS

With the help of computers, everything changed. Well, to be truthful about it, many things changed slowly over many years. Today, in companies that are using the capabilities offered by their computers, the same process of filing resumes and filling a job vacancy might look something like this.

Now resumes are fed through an electronic scanner (more on this in a minute) and are "filed" in computers instead of in filing cabinets. Today's manager who needs a new employee still makes a phone call or sends a requisition form describing the positions and the ideal candidate to a department that is probably called Human Resources instead of Personnel, but something very different happens after that.

Instead of rummaging around in file drawers looking for resumes, today's Human Resources Assistant sits down at a computer, inputs the requirements for the new employee and then watches the computer screen as a list of qualified candidates appears within seconds. Behind each of those names is a resume, which can be called instantly to the screen as well. After a quick appraisal from the person at the keyboard, these resumes are sent electronically to the computer of the manager who requested them. Whenever the manager has the time, he or she can look over the resumes and begin to invite candidates in for interviews.

Computers have revolutionized the ways in which resumes are stored and retrieved today. For the most part,

file cabinets filled with resumes are a thing of the past. And although you can't be sure that the company that receives your resume will "file" it electronically, you have to assume that this is a definite possibility.

That means that you have to understand exactly how computers can "read" your resume and match it up with job openings. Once you understand this, you can write a resume that is easy for a computer to read. And once you write a "computer friendly" resume, you will greatly increase the chances that yours will be one of the resumes that gets selected by that Human Resources Assistant who is looking for resumes to pass along to the manager who is ready to hire a new employee.

You're probably wondering how computers can take job descriptions from managers and find the resumes that are stored inside them. "How exactly do they do that?" you might be asking. It's a very good question—and the answer has a real impact on how you should construct your resume. To understand the answer, you have to know a little bit (but only a little) about how the words on your resume are filed in a computer. This is where "scanning" comes in.

SCANNING ALLOWS COMPUTERS TO "READ"

A "scanner" is a machine that "digitizes" the words and images on pieces of paper so that they can be used in a computer. Scanners are closely related to fax machines. Both make an electronic copy of a page of typed, written, or drawn words or images and then transmit that electronic copy. In the case of fax machines, they usually send the electronic copy to another fax machine. Scanners send the copy to a computer. Once it is in the computer, the information from the copy can be stored in a variety of ways so that it can be retrieved easily when it is needed.

Scanning isn't a foolproof process. Things can (and do) go wrong. If you have ever received a fax that is hard to read, you have seen the kinds of problems that scanners can have. Whole pages can sometimes look out of focus. Words can be "fuzzy" and individual letters can be broken up to the point where they are hard to decipher. And if you think that you have trouble reading a bad fax, you can imagine the problems that computers have in trying to read the same material. For all their celebrated intelligence, computers still can't think. They have to make do with "artificial intelligence" because they don't have brains. And they still have more trouble than humans do when it comes to making sense out of fuzzy letters and words.

The fact that scanners and computers are not perfect readers has some direct implications for your resume. Once you understand that their "reading" skills are limited, you can develop a resume that stands a better chance

of being scanned successfully—that is, with as few errors as possible.

The following tips will help you to produce a resume that is easy for scanners and computers to understand. In general, it pays to remember that you are a better reader than any piece of electronic gear. If your resume is difficult for you to read, it will be even more difficult for the hardware that is trying to make sense out of it for your prospective employer.

TIPS FOR CREATING A "SCANNABLE RESUME"

1. **Use a Simple Typeface.** Whether or not you do your own typing, you still have a choice of type styles for your resume. You want to select one that is "clean and simple." Your resume isn't the place to show off that bizarre new typeface you discovered that looks like it was drawn with chalk by a small child. This might get you noticed by the human who opens the envelope that holds your resume, but it is more likely to get your resume tossed into the nearest wastebasket than entered into the computerized applicant tracking systems that employers are using today.

Here's a quick lesson on typefaces. The styles that seem to have little "feet" at the bottom or little "hats" at the top of most of their letters are known as "serif" (pronounced "sare if") typefaces. Those without these little additions are known as "sans-serif" (pronounced "sahns sare if") type-faces.

Most computerized systems "read" sans serif typefaces better than they read serif faces. There is a smaller chance of running into problems if you use a sans-serif typeface. Samples of each are provided below so that you know what to look for when you are selecting a typeface yourself or speci-fying a face for someone else who is typing your resume. Also below you will find samples of two serif typefaces that are used frequently enough that they will probably be read successfully by most scanners.

This is a sample of a "serif" typeface. Note the "feet" and "hats" that some of the letters contain. These sometimes confuse scan-ners and computers.

This is a sample of a "sans-serif" typeface. Note that the letters in these words don't contain any decorations that might confuse a scanner or computer.

This is a sample of a type-face called Courier. Note how closely it resembles the type that typewriters traditionally used. Because it is so com-mon, most scanners have been programmed so that they can read this typeface.

This is a sample of a typeface called Helvetica. It has a long history

and remains very popular—popular enough, in fact, that most scanners have been programmed so that they can read this typeface.

2. **Don't Use Tiny Type.** Here's a simple rule of thumb: if the type on your resume is hard for you to read, it will be hard for a computer to "read." This means that if you have to strain to read your own resume, the scanner is going to have trouble translating your words for the computer. Don't take a chance. Use a type size that is clearly readable.

This is a sample of type that is too small. It is called "8 point" type.

This is a sample of type that is as small as most people (and most computers) can read easily. It is "10 point."

This is a sample of type that is easy to read. It could be used throughout a resume, if space allows. It is "12 point."

If you type your resume yourself or find someone to do it for you, be sure to specify a typeface that is at least "10 point" in size. This is a simple thing to do these days, and you will be happy that you were smart enough to attend to this detail. Type of this size is very likely to remain readable in all of the formats into which your resume might be put: faxed, electronically scanned, photocopied, and just read at a desk by a human (who will appreciate the fact that your resume doesn't cause undue eyestrain).

3. **Don't Condense Your Type.** You might have noticed, perhaps in reading magazines or books, that type is sometimes set so that words almost run together on every line. This is because the type has been "condensed." The space between every letter has been reduced. You might be tempted to try this on your resume, so that you can fit more words onto a page. Don't give in to this temptation! Scanners are easily confused by condensed type.

This is an example of type that has been condensed. Note how the spaces between letters and words have been reduced.

This is an example of type that is normally spaced. Note how much easier it is to read.

Computerized typesetting systems can be adjusted to condense type, but be sure to tell your typesetter (whether it's another person or your own computer) to avoid condensing. (If you're looking for a phrase that communicates this to both humans and computers, try "Keep the type loose" and you'll have a good chance of getting the result you want.)

4. **Leave Space Between Lines.** Another trick that is sometimes used to fit more type onto a page is to cut down on the amount of space between lines. Again, you might be tempted to try this trick on your resume, especially if you are trying to cram a lot of information into a small space. This is another temptation to avoid. As with leaving out space between letters, leaving out space between lines confuses scanners and invites trouble for your resume.

This is an example of what happens to the paragraph above when the space between lines is reduced:

Another trick that is sometimes used to fit more type onto a page is to cut down on the amount of space between lines. Again, you might be tempted to try this trick on your resume, especially if you are trying to cram a lot of information into a small space. This is another temptation to avoid. As with leaving out space between letters, leaving out space between letters confuses scanners and invites trouble for your resume.

If you want to be sure that you are giving the correct instructions to anyone who might be typing your resume for you, just say that you want "normal line spacing." Because computerized typesetting systems have to be specially adjusted to provide any setting other than "normal," you shouldn't have a problem here.

5. **Don't Underline (And Be Careful With Any Lines.** Before computers (at least before the advent of computerized applicant tracking systems), it was common to find underlining used on resumes. Often it was used to emphasize important facts. Sometimes it was used in place of italic type, to set apart titles or names. Those days are gone! Today, underlining strains the capabilities of scanners and computers. They just

don't understand the point of underlining. And if they don't understand it, they won't accept it. There's no reason to risk computer rejection by underlining anything in your resume.

In addition, while you're thinking like a computer, remember to leave out lines altogether. That means leaving out lines that serve a decorative function, like creating a border around the edge of your resume or putting a box around your name. You have to face the fact that computers don't like decorative lines (even if you do). When in doubt, leave them out.

6. **Use Capital Letters for Emphasis.** Underlining is out, but capital letters are OK. Scanners and computers know how to "read" words that are written in capital letters. If you want to emphasize something in your resume, you can put it into capital letters. Of course, you're doing this only for the humans who will see your resume, since computers are not impressed by words that are written entirely in capitals. To a computer, it's the same word, all caps or upper/lower case.

7. **Boldface Type "Yes"! Italics "No"!** You have probably figured out by now that computers have limited "reading skills." That's because they have to be programmed to recognize every letter in every typeface that they are likely to encounter. As you can imagine, this programming is a massive task. Because it takes a lot

of time, it's quite expensive. Although many typefaces are now easily understood, it's just too costly to try to program recognition of every available face. Since boldface type uses the same type styles as regular type (just a little "heavier" or "thicker"), computers generally manage quite well with it.

However, italic type looks like a completely different set of characters, and computers are often baffled by it. You can see by the samples below why italic type is baffling. Use boldface type for emphasis, but skip italics altogether.

This is what boldface type looks like. It stands out nicely and is still easy to read.

This is what italic type looks like. You can see how confusing these slanted letters can be.

8. **Don't Use Graphics or Ornaments.** In resumes that are designed for human eyes, one way to stand out from the crowd is to use some sort of ornamentation: maybe an unusual typeface for your name or starbursts next to your key qualifications. Perhaps you have emphasized parts of your resume with asterisks or introduced them with "bullets."

Unfortunately, when it comes to scanning your resume into a computer, these techniques backfire. Here is one place where you want your resume to "blend in with the crowd." It's only the words that count in the new computerized arena, so drop the "bells and whistles" and use an all-type resume.

9. **Don't "Box" Your Type.** In the days before tracking systems, another way to highlight areas on a resume was to put a box around important words, or to put a band of gray behind them, or even to print the words in white in a band of solid black. That's not a useful technique today. Boxing and shading can be attractive to human eyes, but they're likely to overtax a scanner and computer. It's better to leave them out of your resume design.

10. **Be Careful with Abbreviations.** Abbreviations are tricky. Some are so common that every computer has been programmed to recognize them (like the two-letter codes that the U.S. Postal Service has assigned to identify states). Some are common, but have a confusing array of presentations (is that basic college degree a BA, a B.A., an AB, an A.B., or a Bach. of Arts?). Others are specific to individual occupations (UNIX, VAX, MPX in the computer field for example). Still others are acronyms for professional associations, which can be perplexing too (is AMA the American Medical Association or the American Marketing Association?).

It's fine to use abbreviations on your resume, but you might want to spell out the full term too if you're not sure that a prospective employer (or an employer's computer) will know what the abbreviation stands for.

There is one more essential tip: Don't Panic! If you can't tell one typeface from another or if you can't tell the difference between boldface and italic type, don't worry. Try to follow the guidelines above but remember that computers don't work without humans to control them. Every company that scans your resume has a person sitting at the scanner whose job it is to look at each resume on the computer after it goes through the scanner. He or she gets paid to "clean up" that computerized resume so that it looks as much like the original resume as possible. Because these "verifiers" want to keep their jobs, they take their work seriously and try to eliminate as many mistakes as they can.

It's also true that technology is improving quickly. Scanning resumes and storing them in computers is a fairly new idea. The fact that it is also a good idea—one that promises to save money and increase efficiency for the companies that use it—means that a lot of effort is being put into this new technology.

The scanning/storing process is constantly improving. Computers can "read" much better today than they could only two years ago. Next year they will be even smarter than they are today. All of this means that the chances of having your resume scanned successfully are increasing.

However, you will still have an advantage over other job seekers if you pay attention to the guidelines above.

HOW RESUMES ARE RETRIEVED WHEN THEY'RE NEEDED

Now that you know that "scanning" allows your resume to be electronically stored in computer databases, you're probably wondering about the next part of this system. How do resumes get selected when there is a job available? Specifically, how is your resume found when you meet the qualifications for a position in a company that has your resume "on file" in its computer?

In most companies, supervisors still start the process that leads to retrieving resumes from computer databases. When they anticipate having a position available in their area, they tell someone in the Human Resources department (the department that used to be called "Personnel").

They usually do this on a requisition form of some sort—a form that asks relevant questions about the position itself and about the kinds of individuals who are most desirable as candidates to be interviewed. The supervisor is encouraged to describe both the job and the ideal candidates in detail, since this increases the chances of finding well-qualified people to interview.

Back in the days when "Personnel Assistants" still searched through file drawers, they took these requisition forms and started hunting for resumes in cabinets. These days, it's more likely that a "Human Resources Specialist" will turn to a computer screen and start typing in the description of the perfect candidate, hoping that he or she is already in the database and waiting to be discovered.

Before computers, the search for resumes could be tedious and time-consuming. Often it didn't pay off. It was a hit-or-miss proposition—and it was more likely to miss than to hit, frequently turning up no resumes of genuinely qualified (and available) candidates. Today, the search can be done in a few seconds, with a good chance of payoff.

"KEYWORDS" ARE THE KEY

Computers aren't really very smart. They can't actually think or reason. But, with decent programming, they can search through huge numbers of words and find exactly the ones that they have been told to find.

Hunting through tens of thousands, or even millions, of words is something that computers can do with terrific speed and accuracy. This ability makes computers eminently well suited to find the resumes of job applicants in databases that contain hundreds or thousands of resumes. All they need to do their work is clear instruction. That's where those job requisitions come in. And that's what leads to the all-important "keywords."

The computerized search process isn't terribly complex. Basically, the computer is asked to find specific words or phrases or abbreviations that match those that were written on the requisition form by the supervisor who is looking for a new employee.

To make the search process more efficient, and therefore faster, the requirements might have been put into "fields" like Level of Education, Certification, Experience, etc. But, fundamentally, the computer is looking for words. And looking for words is something that computers do very well (and very quickly). The words and phrases and abbreviations that they search for are called "keywords."

If you think about it, you can see that the more closely the words and phrases on your resume match the keywords of the computer's search, the greater the odds are that your resume will selected. And if you think about it for another minute, you'll realize that you can definitely improve your chances if you use the same keywords in your resume that the computer will use in its hunt.

But, you might be asking, how can I know what keywords the computer will be trying to find? And how can I be sure I use the same keywords in my resume? Look at the tips that follow!

PUTTING "KEYWORDS" TO WORK FOR YOU

Since keywords are crucial to your success in computerized applicant tracking systems, it is essential that they appear in your resume. The good news is that many of them are probably there already, if you have written a resume. More good news is that it won't take extraordinary efforts on your part to pack your resume full of them, even if you have never written a resume before.

An entire chapter of this book is devoted to helping you identify the keywords that are likely to be used in descriptions of jobs that you want. That chapter will help you develop your own list of keywords that can be strategically placed into your resume.

Here are some straightforward suggestions on how to include these vital keywords in your resume.

1. **If You Have a Job Description, Use It!** If you are applying for a specific position, and you have a description of the position, you possess many of the keywords already! That job description, whether it comes from a newspaper ad, a letter from a friend, or directly from the Human Resources Department, is a goldmine.

It is very likely to use many of the keywords that will later be entered into a computer when the electronic search for candidates is conducted. Since your resume will be scanned exactly as you write it, make sure that you include as many keywords as you can!

If the job description includes the phrase "Bachelor's degree required," be sure to use the phrase in your resume (although you should also include the same information in other ways too, just in case the computer is told to search differently). In this case, your resume might say: "Bachelor's degree in English. B.A., University of Texas." If the job description uses abbreviations, use the same abbreviations in your resume (but, again, spell out the full name if you think that the computer search might be conducted using the full name).

For example, if the job description says "Must be familiar with TQM," your resume might state: "Familiar with TQM (Total Quality Management)." If there are specific product names in the job description, include those names in your resume.

Here's one example: "Requires knowledge of WordPerfect, Word for Windows, and Lotus." You would want to include the identical phrase in your resume: "Knowledge of WordPerfect, Word for Windows, and Lotus." You could then go on to list other software packages that you know how to use, but you will have included the keywords exactly as they were written in the description.

2. **If You Don't Have a Job Description, "Think Like an Employer."** You may not have an exact job description, but you obviously know a few things about any job for which you are submitting a resume. Before you develop your resume, spend a few minutes listing the key requirements of the job you hope to get. (This is one of the goals of the chapter on keywords that comes up later in this book.)

Be as specific as possible. Do you have to type a certain number of words per minute (wpm)? Is certification required? Do you need a college degree? To make your list, "think like an employer." What is your future employer likely to be looking for in an employee? You might go so far as to write out a job description yourself, and then write a resume that responds directly to that description—including the keywords!

Remember, too, that job descriptions are usually available from the company that has a job opening. All you have to do is ask for one. If you don't know where to start, contact the Human Resources or Personnel department. If you need it in a hurry, ask if they can fax it to you—or stop in and pick up a copy. It's definitely worth the effort!

3. **Learn the "Keywords" in Your Field and Use Them in Your Resume!** Every occupation has its "buzzwords," abbreviations, and acronyms. If you think about it, you prob-

ably know lots of them that are specific to the type of work you do (or want to do). These are "keywords" and they need to be included in your resume. It will pay off to make a list of these before you start writing a resume. (One of the best ways to make this list is to use the worksheets in the upcoming chapter on keywords.)

If you don't know the field very well, there are at least two steps that you might want to take:

1) talk to someone who is already employed and knows the jargon;

2) take a look at advertisements for available jobs. Your task is simple: you want to find out what the keywords are. You want to know which words are going to turn up on that requisition form (the one that starts the search process), so that you can use those same words on your resume.

WHAT HAPPENS WHEN THE COMPUTER SELECTS YOUR RESUME?

Computerized applicant tracking systems are designed not only to store and retrieve resumes, but also to send resumes directly to the managers who have requested them. As you have probably guessed, the computerized keyword search produces a list of candidates who meet the search criteria. The person who is conducting the computerized search then looks at the electronically stored resume of each

candidate to verify that he or she does, in fact, have the necessary background and qualifications to fill the available position.

Next, the electronic resumes are forwarded to the manager who will select the candidates to be interviewed. They can be printed out in their entirety and passed along on paper, or they can be sent electronically so that they are available on the manager's computer when he or she is ready to look them over. (Depending on the system being used, there may also be a summary version of each resume available, which allows the manager to retrieve the entire resume with a few commands to the computer.)

Of course, you want to be selected by the computer AND by the manager who will be doing the interviewing for the job. This means that your resume has to be written with both the computer and the manager in mind. It has to observe all of the rules for scanning success spelled out earlier in this chapter. It has to include "keywords" that are likely to be used in the computerized search process. And it has to present you in an appealing way to a manager who may see your resume only on a computer screen!

This is a lot to ask of a resume, but it is entirely possible for you to design your resume so that it accomplishes every one of these tasks. It is the goal of this book to help you do just that.

TIPS FROM A HUMAN RESOURCES SPECIALIST

In his capacity as a Human Resources Specialist for PeopleSoft, a national recruiting firm that places recruitment ads and solicits resumes for a variety of companies across the country, David Bernstein sees hundreds of resumes a day. All have been sent in response to ads that People Soft has placed. At the time David was interviewed, there were 45 ads running in newspapers throughout the U.S. PeopleSoft is committed to scanning every one of those hundreds of resumes the same day that it is received, so David's description of feeling like he is in "the Grand Central Station of resumes" sounds pretty accurate.

PeopleSoft is quite clear in its ads that each one of the resumes that it receives will be electronically scanned and entered into a computerized storage and retrieval system. However, many applicants don't understand what this means and they submit resumes that look fine on paper but end up being rejected by the scanner. Those people are sent postcards telling them that their resumes did not scan successfully and suggesting that they rewrite their resumes to be more compatible with electronic databases. Needless to say, these people lose critical time in the application process—and have a lot of work to do on their resumes! They could have saved time and effort by following the advice in this book.

What follows are suggestions from a professional for anyone who is developing a resume that will be electronically scanned and entered into an applicant tracking system.

1. **Use White Paper.** Although some colors of paper don't confuse the scanner, why take a chance? Use black type on white paper and you will give your resume the best odds of being easily scanned.

2. **Don't Fax Your Resume.** Since you know that there is a chance, with almost any available job, that your resume will be scanned and stored in a computer, don't take chances. If you have ever received a fax, you know how bad the printing can be. There are many reasons why a fax can be "degraded" during transmission, but the point is that a faxed copy is never as good as the original. And scanning a faxed copy is never as good as scanning an original.

Some day it may be possible to fax directly to a scanner, and avoid the paper copy altogether, but that day is still in the future. In the present, don't fax your resume!

3. **Use Type that is Large Enough to Read Easily.** As a person who sees hundreds of resumes a day, David suggests using type of at least 10-point size. Anything smaller is difficult for both scanners and for humans to read. He points out that there is no limit to the length of your

resume once it has been converted into an electronic document, since pages are only a paper concept. So don't worry about how long your resume is; make the type large enough!

4. **Use Standard Size Paper Printed on One Side.** Although it's true that the computer doesn't care how long your resume is, the scanner cares how long your paper is. It is set up to scan 8 1/2" X 11" paper and that is how your resume should be printed.

5. **Don't Fold Your Resume.** The resume you provide is the resume that will get scanned. If it is folded, even once or twice to fit into an envelope, it is quite possible that it will give the scanner problems. If the fold lines run across your lines of type, the letters on those lines are more difficult for the scanner to decipher clearly.

What's the solution? Use an envelope that is large enough to contain your resume without folding. Envelopes that are 9" x 12" are readily available at stationery stores.

6. **Don't Use Graphics of Any Kind.** David confirms that the scanner has trouble dealing with anything other than type. It is programmed specifically to read type, not graphic images. He recommends that resumes contain no borders (even simple line borders), no boxes, no designs, no pictures, and no background images behind type. "Frankly," he says, "the scanner even has trouble figuring out what

asterisks are. It's better to leave out everything except standard type."

7. **Use a Laser Printer.** In the chapter on printing your resume, we will deal further with your options, but if you are using a computer to produce your own resume, be sure to use a laser printer. The type that is reproduced by a dot matrix printer is made up of many little dots (instead of complete letters) and the image quality is not good enough to be scanned with 100% accuracy. If you have someone else type your resume, be sure the final output is done on a laser printer.

8. **Put Your Name in the Upper Left Corner.** "Probably the biggest error that I see, when it comes to scanning," says David, "is that people put the name and address in the middle of their resumes." He adds that "the scanner we use does much better if the name and address are in the top left corner of the resume."

9. **Be Sure to Include Your Skills.** David points out that the first keyword search is a search for specific skills. These are often, as you would expect, the skills that were specified in the ad or job description for an available position. He recommends that all job seekers check their resumes to see that they include skills—especially those that turn up frequently in ads.

10. **The Software is Getting Smarter.** The computer programs that make sense out of electronically

scanned text are getting more sophisticated. As an example, David notes that PeopleSoft routinely searches for "Bachelor of Science in Computer Science" in 12 different ways, all in a matter of seconds. He doesn't think that candidates need to guess at all of the ways the computer might be searching for any piece of information. Including the information in one or two commonly-used ways on a resume should be sufficient.

"Software packages are pretty hip these days about recognizing abbreviations and acronyms, so people shouldn't have to write them twelve different ways themselves. We'll pick them up."

CONCLUSION

There is an acronym from the computer industry that is worth considering when you are developing your resume: "GIGO." It stands for "garbage in = garbage out." If your resume is disorganized, difficult to read, filled with misspellings, or just plain unimpressive, it won't get any better (or any more impressive) when it is scanned into a computer! If your resume doesn't represent you well on paper, it won't represent you well on a computer screen.

You have a head start on other job seekers who haven't read this book and don't know about computerized applicant tracking systems and their electronically scanned resume storage and retrieval capabilities. But you still have to develop a resume that "sells" you to your prospective employers. So keep reading and you will be able to write a resume that works for you!

This chapter has discussed computerized applicant tracking systems— the systems that are being used in rapidly increasing numbers of companies throughout the world. You have learned the basics of how resumes are scanned, filed, and retrieved in these computer systems. This is essential information for job-seeking today!

With your new knowledge, you are better prepared to write a resume that "wins" in the computerized search. Your goal is to be selected by the computer and to have your name and resume forwarded to the manager who is looking for a new employee. You have the basic information you need to write a winning resume. The rest of this book will help you to write that resume.

CHAPTER 2

JOB DATABANKS

COMPUTERS AS MATCHMAKERS

Computers have made it possible to store and retrieve vast amounts of information quickly—and with great accuracy. For job seekers, one of the most significant results of new technologies has been the establishment of "databanks" filled with jobs. The scope of these job databanks is often national and sometimes international. These "banks" of jobs allow employers to list available positions and they allow people looking for work to discover these positions—in addition, they frequently allow applicants to have their resumes transmitted directly to prospective employers: on paper, by fax, or even electronically.

Job databanks are maintained by large corporations, by profit-making services like recruitment firms, and by not-for-profit organizations like professional associations. There are also computerized databanks filled with the resumes of job-seekers. These are designed to be accessed by employers who have job openings and want to "browse" through listings of available candidates, perhaps before they begin advertising a vacancy.

Whatever specific form job databanks may take, they have a number of features in common. At their most basic, they store information on candidates and jobs, and then provide a computerized "matching service." To enter a job databank, candidates submit a resume (on paper or electronically) or they fill out an application form (again, either on paper or electronically). Sometimes they do both.

Resumes submitted on paper are usually "scanned" by an electronic scanner and their text is digitized so that it can be "read" by a computer. Resumes submitted electronically are also "read" electronically. Application forms are designed so that their information can be easily entered into the computerized database.

FINDING JOB DATABANKS

If you are looking for a job, it can be worthwhile to investigate job databanks. There are several places you can begin your investigation. To find commercial services, check the classified advertising sections of major metropolitan newspapers, especially the Sunday editions. You can also look at classified ad sections of national papers, such as *USA Today*, *The Wall Street Journal*, and *Dow Jones Business Employment Weekly*.

To locate not-for-profit databanks, start with the professional associations of the occupations that interest you. If you don't already belong to a professional association, or if you are not sure which associations represent your job field, spend a few minutes with the *Encyclopedia of Associations*. It's available in nearly all libraries and it contains a wealth of information for job seekers.

In addition, don't forget to check any publications in your job field that contain employment listings. This includes newsletters and magazines that are intended for people who are already employed in an occupational area.

Some fields that employ large numbers of people (computer programming for example) have numerous commercial publications (like magazines and even newspapers) that are devoted to the field. These often contain ads for job databanks, or ads that are placed by databanks for employers that are taking advantage of the recruiting and matching capabilities that databanks offer. However, even if your occupational area has only a small number of trade publications, it is still worth checking their advertising sections to look for databanks.

A number of job databanks are available "on-line." These are discussed in more detail in the next chapter, which is devoted to using the Internet as part of a job search. The databanks described in this chapter are often maintained specifically to

serve the recruitment needs of corporations and are not available to be "browsed" by individual job seekers.

Once you have located a job databank, it's time to start asking questions. There is a list of questions below, and it's important to get answers to as many of these questions as possible.

Most databanks are in business to make money (with the obvious exception of those maintained by not-for-profit organizations). Nearly all charge fees to job seekers. The fastest and simplest way for a job databank to make money is to sign up as many fee-paying job seekers as possible. This benefits the backers of the databank, but it doesn't always benefit the job seekers.

If you are a job seeker, you want to know how likely it is that your resume (or "profile") will be sent to a prospective employer who has an appropriate job to fill. You want, in other words, a databank that will work for you—one that will link you up with potential jobs! Most databank services have brochures available that describe their services and outline their fees. These are yours for the asking, so be sure to ask. Some offer information by phone, which is convenient, but not as binding as putting the information into print. Some ask job seekers to sign agreements. It goes without saying that any agreement should be carefully scrutinized before it is signed.

Here is a list of questions to ask of any databank service. There may be other questions that are important to you, and you should be sure to get answers to all of your questions before you register with such a service.

QUESTIONS FOR JOB DATABANKS

1. What are your services?
2. How do your services typically work for most of your customers?
3. What are your fees?
4. What can I expect to receive for the fees I pay?
5. How long will my resume remain "active" in your system?
6. Where can I expect my profile to be sent?
7. Do employers list job openings with your databank?
8. Do employers list openings exclusively with you?
9. What guarantees do you offer to job seekers who register with you?
10. Approximately how many candidates are in your system—and how many employers regularly access the system?
11. Can you assess my chances of being referred to an employer for a job?
12. What are your refund policies?

HOW TO APPLY

In the information you receive from a job databank, there will be instructions on how to apply. If there is an agreement to be signed, be sure to read it carefully so that you understand

its terms. If you are submitting your resume to be electronically scanned, check it first against the section "Guidelines for Scanned Resumes" later in this chapter (you might also want to read about scanning in the previous chapter on applicant tracking systems).

If you are completing an application form, study the information included below under the heading "How Do Job Databanks Work?" If you are sending a resume electronically, look over the suggestions in "How to Send Your Resume Electronically."

HOW DO JOB DATABANKS WORK?

Because computers can store vast amounts of information and retrieve it on command, they are well suited for the tasks performed by job databanks. Databank systems are "matchmakers." They match candidates with available jobs and they match jobs with available candidates. The computerized search depends on making matches that are as exact as possible (people have the ability to sense "near matches," but computers don't).

Generally, matches are made by "field" of information (like years of experience, previous job titles, specific skills, etc.). This is why application forms are, in some ways, easier for job databanks to handle, since job seekers answer questions or fill in blanks that become "fields" for searching. Resumes that are electronically scanned may be searched on "keywords" (more on this below).

Before you complete an application form, familiarize yourself with the most important qualifications of people in your occupation. One simple way to do this is to study classified ads. See which words and terms appear regularly. You're doing research to find out what employers want so that you can use the same words and phrases (if they actually describe you) when you fill out the application form. Since you know in advance that computers will try to make an exact match, you're increasing your chances that an exact match will be made with you!

ELECTRONICALLY SCANNED RESUMES

Scanning is discussed at length in the previous chapter on applicant tracking systems. To summarize here, scanning allows your resume to be entered into a computerized job databank, with all of its words and phrases intact. When a search of resumes in a databank is conducted, it is done by "keywords." The computer tries to find the same words and phrases in your resume that have been entered as keywords. It's actually an easy task for a computer.

For job seekers, this process demonstrates the importance of being familiar with the "buzzwords" of your occupation. If these words and phrases appear in your resume, you increase your chances of being "matched" in a computer's search. (The chapter on "keywords" is devoted to helping you identify keywords for the types of jobs you are seeking.)

Electronic scanning is not a perfect process. The software that allows a computer to "read" is not flawless. You can increase the chances of your resume being scanned successfully by following the guidelines below. Before you send your resume to a job databank, check it against these guidelines. For more complete information on the guidelines, see the previous chapter.

GUIDELINES FOR SCANNED RESUMES

1. **Use a simple typeface.** Your goal is not to impress a human reader with your typographic design skills. The goal is to have every word "read" by a computer.

2. **Don't use tiny type.** Don't cram a page full of small type. It is just too difficult for a scanner to "read."

3. **Don't condense your type.** Avoid the temptation to squeeze words onto lines or onto the page as a whole. Scanners need to "see" words individually and not run together.

4. **Leave space between lines.** This also helps scanners input information into a computer.

5. **Don't underline.** Underlining makes no sense to a scanner. You should avoid lines altogether, including borders and decoration.

6. **Capital letters are OK**. This is one way to make things stand out for humans while not confusing computers.

7. **Boldface type "yes"! Italics "no"!** Another way to highlight words for people without overwhelming scanners is to use boldface type (still in a simple typeface). Don't use italic typefaces, because these will baffle many scanners.

8. **Don't use graphics or ornaments.** Leave out any unusual decorative elements in a resume that may be scanned. Scanners are not programmed to recognize anything other than straightforward typefaces.

9. **Don't "box" your type.** Avoid using bands of gray, or putting boxes around type, or "dropping out" white type from a black background. Stick to black type on white paper.

10. **Be careful with abbreviations.** Computers understand the most common abbreviations in most job fields, but if you are unsure about how easily recognized a specific abbreviation might be, spell out the whole word or phrase and then include the abbreviation (or vice versa). Give the computer a choice.

HOW TO SEND YOUR RESUME ELECTRONICALLY

Many job databanks allow you to send your resume electronically. This method holds the appeal of very rapid transmission, meaning that your resume can be received within a few seconds instead of the few days it would take by conventional mail. It also offers the opportunity to have your resume entered into the databank completely intact, without any of the errors that can be inserted by scanning.

If you have access to a computer that connects to the global "electronic mail" network (even if it doesn't have full access to the Internet), you can successfully send your resume electronically.

Job databanks that accept resumes electronically usually provide instructions on how to transmit your resume. These should be easy to follow. However, there are a couple of things that they may not tell you that are important for you to know.

1) **Your resume needs to be stripped of all of its "formatting codes."** These are the codes that are inserted by word processing software that tell where paragraphs begin or which type is boldface type, for example. Databanks prefer that you remove these codes yourself, but they can also do it for you (which involves more time and labor, but probably no

27

extra charge).

Most word processing packages include the option of removing these codes. If you want to do this yourself, or if the databank requires it, your word processing documentation or "help line" will usually tell you how to accomplish the task. You might also check with friends and colleagues to see if they can be of assistance. One "buzz phrase" to use with computer-literate friends is "converting a text file to ASCII." This phrase should give them an idea of what you are trying to do.

2) **Since all of the formatting codes will be missing, all that will be left is words** (and punctuation marks). This fact alone changes the way you should look at your resume, because at this point it is no longer a "document." It is not a sheet of paper with words on it. Instead, it is a collection of words and phrases that can be "read" by a computer. Of course, this puts a greater emphasis on the words you have chosen to use in your resume. Before you transmit your resume electronically, try to envision it this way—try to see it as a computer will see it.

Once more, the importance of "keywords" is underscored. Again, it is crucial that the words and phrases that appear in job descriptions and advertisements for the kind of job you want also appear in your resume. If you are applying for a specific job, and you have a description of the position,

take a few minutes to look through your resume to see if the EXACT WORDS AND PHRASES are there. If they're not, and you can legitimately add them, do it!

If a description of the ideal candidate is also noted in the job description, and you can honestly claim to have all or some of the same skills, experience, or other stated qualifications, it's definitely worth the time to re-word your resume so that it includes the EXACT WORDS AND PHRASES that appear in the job description. The chapter on "keywords" goes into this at greater depth and provides a worksheet to use in developing your own personal list of keywords.

Try to respond to each statement in a job description if possible. The more precisely your qualifications match those of the ideal candidate (the one who offers absolutely everything that the employer wants), the greater the chances that the computer's search will select you!

"ONCE YOU'RE IN, YOU'RE IN"

One great advantage of computerized job databanks is that your resume remains "on file" and can be discovered in any search that might be requested by employers or recruiters with jobs to fill. This means that you may be considered for many more jobs than the single position for which you applied. And this is great news!

Unlike the paper-in-filing cabinets

"systems" that were used in times B.C. (Before Computers), today's electronic filing systems really work. They can survey the equivalent of dozens of file drawers filled with resumes in just a few seconds—and they can list the most qualified candidates or provide instant access to candidates' resumes.

In B.C. times, being told that your resume was being kept "on file" could mean that it was about as likely to be found as if it had been shredded. Today if you're told that your resume is "in the computer" or "in the database," it could be a cause for joy.

This potential for discovery is one reason that some databanks charge by a time period to keep your resume "active" in the system. Be sure to ask about such fees, which could be assessed by the month, by the quarter of a year, etc. Databanks are not like file cabinets, and you may decide that it is worth the additional charge to keep your resume active in a system if the system is working for you.

ELECTRONIC COVER LETTERS

When you send your resume electronically, you can usually send a "cover letter," just as if you were applying for a job in a traditional way. At the very least, you will want to identify the position for which you are transmitting your resume and where you saw the position listed or described. You can also include, as you would in a letter, a description of your qualifications for the position. How-

ever, you should realize that your "electronic cover letter" will not accompany your resume into the computer that houses the job databank. In most cases, only your resume (or application) will be entered.

As you can see, this is another reason why it makes sense to include the "keywords" of a job description in your resume. This may mean developing a slightly different resume for each job you're seeking, but it is definitely worth the extra effort. By taking the time to include keywords, you increase the odds that your resume will be "matched" to the job you desire. Knowing this, there is no good reason not to include the keywords. It does require a few minutes of time, but you are probably modifying a resume that is already on a word processor, so the task isn't that difficult or time-consuming.

Remember that employers often receive hundreds of resumes for an advertised job opening. A growing number of job seekers are sending their resumes electronically, so the fact that you are e-mailing yours isn't going to make you a more attractive candidate in itself. And the fact that you have submitted your resume electronically isn't going to reduce the competition either.

Employers still want to know what you have to offer. They want to know how close you are to their ideal candidate. What you say—and how you say it—are what counts. So take the extra time and customize your resume before you fire it off from your computer to the computer that will be used to decide whether you are a qualified candidate. That extra time will pay off by increasing the chances that the computer will determine that you are, in fact, qualified.

Before you transmit your resume to a job databank, or directly to a prospective employer, you might want to review the chapters on "Keywords" and "Cover Letters."

A NOTE ABOUT CONFIDENTIALITY

In using a job databank, it is possible that your resume might be sent to a prospective employer whom you don't want to receive it—like your present employer! Most databanks allow you to list the names of companies that should not receive your resume. If this is an important issue for you, be sure to ask about it before you send your resume to a databank.

To summarize, job databanks can serve a valuable function for job seekers. They hold the possibility of helping candidates to be "matched" with available jobs throughout the U.S. (and around the world). As with all services that are offered to job seekers, it pays to investigate. You will want to find databanks that are most likely to have jobs in your field and you will want to compare the terms of their

contracts or agreements.

However you submit your resume (or application form), take particular care with its wording. Whenever possible, use the "buzzwords" of your occupation and always try to include the exact words and phrases that appear in specific job descriptions when you are applying for specific jobs. With care on your part in selecting a job databank and in submitting your resume for computerization, you may find that job databanks can be an integral part of your job-seeking campaign.

CHAPTER 3

RESUMES AND THE INTERNET

DISCOVERING THE WORLD ON-LINE

Although it's still in the adolescent phase of its development—slightly clumsy and not yet fully formed, but filled with great potential—the Internet promises to be a valuable tool for job seekers. It has the capability of serving as a worldwide "job bank," allowing job hunters across the globe to locate appropriate jobs and then apply for those jobs electronically by transmitting their resumes directly from their personal computers.

Future developments in telecommunications and computing will make such services more widely available, but there are many resources that are accessible right now on the Internet for anyone who is looking for a job. This chapter provides an introduction to some of those resources, but the Internet is a very dynamic, rapidly-changing place and one of the best ways to keep up with it is to "surf" it frequently. Use the information that follows to get your feet wet and then plunge in on your own. You will make some great discoveries, meet some new people, and have some fun along the way. Happy surfing!

GETTING CONNECTED

The Internet isn't really a "thing" or a "place." It's a network. It links thousands of computers around the world, making available the information that is stored on those computers to anyone who is able to find it. (Actually, it doesn't make available every piece of information in every connected computer. The person in charge of each computer decides what will be shared on the Internet.)

From the point of view of an ordinary "surfer" seated in front of a computer in a home or office, though, the Internet appears to be a limitless library. The user doesn't see the tens of thousands of connections that are being made among computers to bring the information into that one home or office. That's the beauty of the Internet. It brings data from around the world directly to individuals. All you need is a computer and a way to connect.

The list of items you need for access to the Internet is short. You will have to have a computer, a modem, a telephone line, communications software, and an access service. Let's look at those one at a time.

Computer: Obviously, you must have a computer. However, you don't need a specific brand or type. And you don't necessarily have to go out and buy a computer if you don't already own one (or if you own one that's not up to the task of accessing the Internet).

It's quite possible that you can gain access to the Internet from a computer that you don't own. There might be a computer at your place of employment that you can use. You might have a friend who is already "on the Net" from home or work who will let you log on there. Nearly all colleges and universities are connected to the Net and many are offering ways for students and non-students to gain access. Increasingly, public libraries are providing patrons with computers that are hooked up to the Internet.

Finally, enterprising entrepreneurs are finding ways to make access available to the public (and make a profit at the same time). These public-access sites are opening in some places that look a little unlikely at first glance, like photocopy shops (especially those that rent computers by the hour), bookstores, and so-called "cyber cafes" that combine offerings of food, beverages (often featuring a mind-jangling array of coffees), and computers.

It pays to look around for creative ways to access the Internet. And it pays to ask around too. Chances are good that someone you know is already accessing the Internet. That person is a good starting point for your search. And call your local library or the library of a nearby college or university. If the library doesn't offer on-line access, ask for a referral to another site that might. Check out the ads in your local newspaper. It's hard to predict where public-access sites will turn up in your community, so keep your eyes open.

If you do own a computer and want to use it to access the Internet, you will want to find out whether it has the capability. One way to find out is to ask a friend who is "into computers." Another is to ask at a computer store. Either way, you will need a complete description of your computer, including its speed (sometimes expressed in the model number, like AST 386SX, often as a "megahertz" number, like 486, or by the name of its processor chip, like Pentium) and its memory (both ROM, short for "ready only memory," and RAM, an abbreviation for "random access memory"). If you don't have this information memorized yourself, take a look at the printed materials that came with your computer or look at the information on the "initialization screens" that come up when you turn your computer on.

You might find that your computer already has the capacities required for accessing the Net. Or you might discover that it can gain the capacities through "upgrades," often by adding memory (which can be as simple as putting a new "card" into the computer). An upgrade might be an affordable way to gain Internet access capability without having to invest in a new computer. It is certainly an option to explore before making the decision to buy another computer.

Modem: If you own a computer and plan to use it to access the Internet, you will need a modem—the device that attaches to your computer (or can be installed in the computer itself) and allows the two-way transmission of data over telephone lines. The speed of transmission is probably the most critical feature of a modem. If you have to buy a modem, and you pay a visit to a computer store, your salesperson will probably advise buying the fastest modem available today. That modem will permit sending and receiving information as speedily as possible. However, the connection service you use to access the Internet is likely to be transmitting data at a rate that is much slower than today's standard, so that it can accommodate the many users who have slower modems.

Because faster modems cost more money, you might want to find out the transmission speed of the access service before you purchase a modem, especially if your main use of the modem will be to connect to the service. Your salesperson might be helpful on this subject, since computer stores often provide free—with the purchase of a modem—software that allows you to connect to an on-line service at no charge for a trial period (which usually consists of several hours of access time).

If you find out that the connection services in your area are transmitting at slower speeds (and are not planning to speed up in the near future), you could buy a slower modem and save some money.

Telephone line: A telephone line is the first link to the Internet. Your modem plugs into a phone line to provide access to the world of information outside your home or workplace. It's quite possible that you can use your existing phone line, but it's smart to check with a computer store and with your phone company to be sure.

During the time that your phone line is connected to your computer, it replaces your telephone, which cannot be used to place or receive calls. If this is a problem, you can have an additional phone line installed, but this can be expensive and it brings with it a separate monthly charge.

Before investing in an additional line, you might want to try using your access service for a few weeks and see whether this inconveniences your family or business enough to warrant the lease of a new line. Remember that most on-line services will give you several hours of access at no charge as a "free trial." This period may be all that you need to discover whether or not you want to install an additional phone line.

Communications software: If you have to buy a modem for your computer, you will also need the software that allows your modem to connect with an Internet access service. If you purchase your modem from a computer store or dealer, you will probably be asked about your intended use, and you will be encouraged to buy the appropriate software at the time you purchase the modem. Often the price of the modem includes the required software.

If you are planning to purchase a modem by phone or mail, be sure to inquire about the cost of the communications software. Sometimes mail order prices that look extremely low do not include this software—and you will find that your modem is essentially worthless without the software.

Access service: Although there are other ways to gain access to the Internet, one of the most widely used methods is the commercial access service. These services usually work by subscription. They charge a monthly use fee, which entitles users to either unlimited access to their resources or a certain number of hours of "connect time." They may charge additional fees for special services or for additional hours of connect time beyond the monthly allotment.

The only other charge is for telephone time. If you have a telephone plan that allows unlimited local calling, and the access service you select has a local phone number, you won't incur additional telephone charges.

However, if your phone company charges you by the minute or "message unit," or if the call to your access service is charged as a long-distance call, you could be shocked by the impact on your phone bill!

Obviously, it's essential to find out this out before you subscribe to a service—and to confirm the information with your telephone company. To borrow a phrase from advertising for a national hotel chain, when it comes to charges for Internet access, "the best surprise is no surprise."

Some of the most popular national access services are listed below, along with their phone numbers. You will probably want to call more than one, since rates and services vary among them. Be sure to inquire about special offers. This is a very competitive business and offers of free services are often included in an introductory offer.

When you call, request an introductory information packet. This usually includes a diskette along with printed information. The packet should be available without charge and it should include all of the terms of service. The service itself usually begins when you insert the diskette into your computer and follow the instructions for use.

Because most services include a free trial use period, you can even try more than one and compare them.

This is an ongoing, monthly investment and you should be satisfied that you have decided on the service that is best for you.

INTERNET ACCESS SERVICES

All of the companies listed below offer access to the Internet. Most offer many other services in addition. You will probably want to contact several in order to compare their services. Be sure to read the section above before enrolling with a service.

America Online: 800-827-6364

Compuserve: 800-848-8990

Delphi: 800-695-4005

Netcom: 800-353-6600

Prodigy: 800-776-3449

ALTERNATIVE ACCESS SERVICES

There are non-profit and non-commercial groups working to provide free or low-cost access to the Internet. If one of your primary hopes in being connected to the Net is to "chat" with other people through your computer, perhaps by sharing information and experiences around looking for a job, you might be interested in an electronic bulletin board service (BBS). These exist for nearly any interest area you can imagine (and some that you would never imagine).

The commercial providers of Internet access, like those listed above, support numerous bulletin boards and allow access to thousands of others. However, there are other services that link bulletin boards and users and some of these provide access to the Internet as well, often at lower prices than the commercial services.

The easiest way to find a BBS of interest to you is to ask a friend who has Internet access now or is currently chatting with others who share the same interests. Anyone you know who is currently "surfing" the Internet can provide you with leads to BBS's, many of which you can access directly through your own computer and modem, even without a connection to the Internet. Some of these could be based near you, so that you might not have to incur long-distance telephone charges to access them.

If you find that you are using BBS's that charge fees or that are only available through long-distance telephone numbers, you might consider accessing them through one of the commercial services, where you will gain access to many other services (and many other bulletin boards) as well.

Just as there are bulletin board services that are available without charge, there are groups that provide free access to the Internet. These are often guided by a philosophical commitment to the free exchange of information. They put that commitment into action by providing a link to a massive repository of information without charge. These so-called "freenets" may have no real administrative staff to speak of, since they can be provided by one person with a home computer and a little time to spare. And they can be found in communities of any size.

Again, the quickest way to find a freenet is to check with friends and colleagues who are "into computers." If there is a freenet in your community, these are the people who will probably know about it. However, you can also contact the National Public Telecomputing Network, which serves as a clearinghouse and association for freenets. Call them directly at 216-498-4050, fax them at 216-498-4051, or write to them at Box 1987, Cleveland, OH 44106.

FINDING JOBS ON-LINE

The Internet does not exist specifically for job seekers, but anyone looking for a job will find a wealth of information on the Internet (and in the commercial access services too). There are "job banks" which list specific available jobs, "career centers" where you can research career fields and even "talk" with a career counselor, employment agencies which promote jobs that are available immediately, complete classified ads from newspapers around the world, and a terrific array of information about companies that could be your next employer.

It is often said by career counselors that it isn't the best-qualified job seekers who get hired into jobs, but the best-informed job seekers. In other words, people who know how to find jobs are the ones who find jobs. Today, the best-informed job seekers include the Internet in their job searches and preparation because it is an immediately-available source of an extraordinary array of information.

With enough time (and a little luck), you can probably find out just about anything you want to know on the Internet without leaving your computer! Want to know the states or cities with the lowest rates of unemployment? How about the cities that have been selected as the "most livable"? Maybe you would like to learn which major national corporations have openings in your job field, and at which of their sites across the country, or even around the world.

Answers to all of these questions (and many more) can be found on the Internet. It will take some time, some patience, and some ingenuity, but the rewards can be great. And your searches can be fun too.

Because the Internet is not a place or a thing, but rather a link among thousands of computers and tens of thousands of databases, users need tools that allow them to search the Internet. And because the Internet is so amorphous and huge, and because its many databases may each have different structures and features, designing these search tools has been particularly difficult.

However, vast amounts of research time and money are being poured into programs that hold the promise of simple Internet searching. These programs are often referred to as "browsers" or "navigators." With the money and time invested will come progress. Within the next few years, a number of products will appear on the market to help make "surfing the Net" a much easier activity than it is today.

Obviously the commercial access services are competing with each other right now to provide uncomplicated access to the Internet. New developments in search software are likely to show up soonest on the commercial services. However, it is also true that you can walk into your local computer store today (or call a mail order supplier) and buy "browsing" software that will make your search for information far easier than it would have been only a year ago.

If you are using your home computer and want to access the Internet without subscribing to a commercial service and without connecting through a local "freenet," it's worth a trip to a computer store. Ask for a demonstration of the latest navigational software for Internet access. Go equipped with all of the facts and figures of your home computer (brand and model number, RAM and ROM

capacities, etc.) and ask if what you see on the computer screen at the store will appear in exactly the same way at home. Remember to ask, too, about the costs of telephone time and other "hidden" charges.

No matter how you connect to the Internet, you will want to conduct searches to find the information you need. To do this, you will use "search words" or phrases. The first to start with are words like "jobs," or "employment," and you can also use phrases like "job lists" or "job listings," "employment agencies," job vacancies" and others of your own choosing. Using these alone will keep you occupied for hours. Luckily, your browsing software will probably allow you to store the "addresses" of the sites that you find to be best for you, so that you can return directly to a site without going through the entire search process each time you log on.

You will also be able to "download" information, transferring it directly into storage on your own computer, as well as being able to print out information that you want to store on paper. With the right hardware connected to your computer, you will find that sites offer sound and sophisticated graphics, sometimes including moving images and animation. For the serious job seeker, these are not essential pieces.

Job seekers want information— and information is what the Internet offers. To find the information you want, start talking with friends and colleagues about what they have found, join on-line "chat groups" of job seekers and start asking questions, and get "surfing" on your own. You will be amazed at how much information you can find!

New Internet sites are created every day, even every hour. Your access service may have a feature that allows you to receive a list of new sites, maybe one that is customized to your interests. If you don't have such a service, you can try connecting to one that provides daily updates.

Using your computer's "e-mail" function, send a message to "majordomo@is.internic.net" and enter as your message "subscribe net-happenings-digest" (leaving the subject line of your e-mail blank). That will result in your receiving a list on your e-mail every day of the sites that have been added over the preceding 24 hours. Once you have these addresses, you can simply enter them into your browser one at a time and find out what information is available at each site. If you like what you find, you can store the address in your personal browser file to make it easy to find again.

CREATIVE JOB HUNTING ON THE INTERNET

If you are looking for work, you have probably heard someone mention the "hidden job market." You have likely figured out that this refers to the thousands of unadvertised jobs that are actually open at any moment. It also refers to the possibility of creating a job for yourself with an employer who needs your services badly enough to create a job for you, even though a position does not exist right now.

The Internet can be a wonderful help in tapping into the hidden job market. Two features in particular are of tremendous interest to job seekers: information databases and electronic mail.

Information databases are one of the most prominent benefits of the Internet. Tens of thousands of computerized databases are available to Internet browsers. And this is great news for job seekers. Not only can you research specific companies and organizations that might offer you a job; you can also discover the names of specific individuals who might make that offer! With the help of electronic mail ("e-mail") you can send letters and resumes directly to the computers of those individuals, without ever using a piece of paper.

If you are a job seeker, you can see instantly the appeal of this. You can target a company that might be a potential employer, research that company, find out the name of an individual to contact, and then contact the person with a letter and resume that are tailored just for that person—and you can ensure that the person receives it directly by computer, completely bypassing the mail and any secretaries that could otherwise stand in your way. This is nothing short of a revolution in job hunting!

If you know the name of the company you want to research, and you have a "browser" as part of your Internet access, you can conduct a search simply by entering the name of the company. Depending upon your browsing software, the list you get may be extraordinarily long—listing every place on the Internet where the company's name appears—or it may be very short—noting those places where substantial descriptions of the company appear. Although it can take some time to find, once you discover a database that provides the kind of information you're looking for, you can store the address of the site so that you can return there directly for your future research on other companies.

If you're like most job seekers, you will want to know about the size of the company, the number of people it employs, the kinds of products or services it produces, and the names of key employees who might be interested in hiring you. All of this information exists in databases on the Internet. It will take a little patience to uncover, but the reward may well be worth the effort. You could probably find the same information through diligent work at a public library, but the data on the Internet is likely to be more current

and easier to unearth—and you never have to leave your computer to find it.

If you have trouble getting the information you want—and friends, colleagues, and relatives can't offer assistance—call your local library and ask to speak with a research librarian. These days a reference librarian has probably had enough experience with the Internet to suggest specific sites for you to "visit." If not, try calling the library at a nearby college or university. The reference librarians there are very likely to be using the Internet regularly and they should be able to offer advice on sites that can provide just the kind of information you need.

Once you have identified companies that look promising, you can make contact by mail—the traditional route—or by electronic mail—the new alternative route. If you know that there is a specific job opening, and you want to apply for it, you can send a cover letter and resume by either method—or by both. If you are trying to uncover a "hidden job" (one that exists but hasn't been advertised or one that might be created just for you), you can still send a cover letter, with or without a resume, but the content should be a little different. Cover letters have their own chapter coming up, but a brief discussion about how to use "e-mail" is important here.

Electronic mail is used to communicate within the workplace and between workplaces, as well as to connect individuals from home computer to home computer. Because many of the messages that are transmitted are between colleagues and friends, a tone of informality has become the norm on e-mail. This has led to an acceptance of such informalities as misspellings, incomplete sentences, improper punctuation, and even grammatical mistakes. While these may be acceptable in e-mail conversations with friends, they are definitely not acceptable in corresponding with potential employers!

As the chapter on cover letters points out in greater detail, your e-mail with someone who may be your next boss must follow standard business practices. Although you may treat all of your e-mail like casual conversations, you must treat your e-mail with employers just like you would treat formal letters that you send by mail (or "snail mail" as e-mail users refer to the U.S. Postal Service).

NETWORKING ON "THE NET"

Using the Internet is a new way to look for a job. Think of it as a supplement to other approaches and not as a replacement for other techniques. In fact, the Internet can support more traditional job-hunting efforts. Here's how. Instead of spending hours studying printed directories that list addresses of corporations, and perhaps some of their employees, you can often find the same information

in seconds on the Net. In addition, you can frequently find e-mail addresses for individuals that you won't find in any printed directory.

By logging on to bulletin board services and by joining chat groups, you can "meet" people around the country, and around the world, who can recommend places to look for work—and even specific people to contact. As every career counselor and job-hunting guidebook will tell you, one vital part of your job search is to build a "network" of contacts. And there is no faster way to create a personal network of contacts than to log onto the Net!

If you are a member of a professional association, a union, a fraternal organization, or any group that shares an interest of yours, it is safe to say that it already has (or is considering) an Internet "site." Because sites are now so easy and inexpensive to establish, even the smallest membership organization can take advantage of this new way to link its members. Of course, every one of those members is a potential contact in your personal "network."

Fortunately, the tone of "conversations" throughout the Internet is "chatty" and this allows you to announce your interest in obtaining a new job and ask for advice and for names of people and companies to contact. Don't be bashful about this. Everyone has to look for work at some time. If this is your time, what better group to turn to than one that shares your interests? And remember that your next job lead could come from someone who shares your favorite hobby just as readily as it might come from a fellow member of a professional association.

There are hundreds of jobs listed every day on the Internet. That's the good news. The bad news is that many of them are jobs in computer-related industries. It's not a surprise that these "high tech" jobs are among the first to be announced on the Net. It makes sense that companies looking for "techies" would turn to this high-tech network.

If you work in any branch of the vast computer industry, you should try to include the Internet in your job-search plans. However, many professional associations, across all occupational fields, regularly post their positions on Internet directories that are accessible to all of their members.

All of the major on-line access services have long lists of "miscellaneous" jobs that anyone who subscribes to the service can browse. If you subscribe, and you're looking for a job, you will want to check out the job listings on your service. And don't forget the classified ads that are reprinted on-line from newspapers around the U.S. Scanning through these, especially if you are thinking of relocating to another city, could really pay off.

RECRUITERS ON "THE NET"

If you are looking for work and looking to the Internet for its listings of job openings, you will soon discover that many of the jobs are listed by employment agencies and professional recruitment firms. This doesn't make the jobs any less real and it shouldn't automatically discourage you from applying. However, a few cautions may be in order.

First, you should make sure that there is truly a match between what you are looking for (and what you have to offer) and the job that you apply for. It is a waste of your time (and the time of a recruiter as well) to apply for jobs that you don't really have a chance of getting. Remember that thousands of other people are reading the same on-line ads that you are and that some very well-qualified individuals are going to apply in competition with you. If you don't have the required background or experience, don't bother to apply.

Second, you will want to find out complete details of the job, including such things as its location, its salary, and the nature of the work. Many employment services offer tantalizing descriptions of positions to entice as many candidates as possible to apply. The reality of the job may not be as rosy as the initial description. You should know in advance that the recruiter who receives your letter or resume (whether you send it by e-mail or "snail mail" or fax) is quite likely to contact you about other jobs as well. And since recruiters actually work for employers, and because they are paid a commission each time one of "their" candidates gets hired, it is to their advantage to refer as many qualified candidates as they can.

In fact, you may not even know that your resume has been forwarded to other employers unless you ask (and you won't know exactly what has been added or deleted from your resume before it was forwarded). You shouldn't be discouraged from applying for jobs that are listed by employment services, but you should know what you might be getting into before you apply.

Third, you will want to clarify that there is no fee involved in applying for a job that is listed by an employment or recruitment firm. Any fees involved should be paid by employers and not by candidates. If there is any kind of fee to be paid by applicants, whatever its guise (as a "processing fee" or "application fee" or a fee by any other name), think twice before applying for the job and paying the fee. Reputable recruitment firms do not charge fees to candidates for the "privilege" of applying for a job.

This advice applies also to firms that offer, for a fee, to send your resume to employers. Although this may be a service that you feel is worth your money, you should know that these "broadcast" resumes forwarded to employers (without actually being solicited by them) are very unlikely to result in a job for you. Again, professional recruitment firms are retained by employers to find outstanding candidates for jobs that they want to fill quickly. Generally, the only fees that are involved are those paid by employers to agencies and there should not be any fees charged to candidates.

In summary, the Internet offers a wonderful new resource for job seekers. There are thousands of actual jobs listed every day. And there is a wealth of information available to everyone who has the patience and creativity to find it and put it to use. If you have access to the Net, and if you are looking for a job, you owe it to yourself to spend some time on-line. Even if you don't find a job directly from your "surfing," you will discover a new universe—and you will probably make some new friends in the process!

CHAPTER 4

"KEYWORDS"

YOUR KEY
TO SUCCESS

If you have read any of the chapters that precede this one, you will have noticed the mention of "keywords." If you haven't read the previous chapters, slow down and read this one! In the age of the electronic resume, keywords are something you have to know.

The concept of keywords is simple. Basically, keywords are the words or phrases used in searching any database of candidates. They are the words or phrases that are entered into a computer to find applicants. They provide a means of "matching" available candidates with available jobs. Obviously, these words are important to job seekers. Keywords can make the difference between being selected or ignored for a job opening.

How can you put keywords to work for you? Actually it's not hard to do. If you have a description of the specific job you want (or even a description of the general type of job you want), you probably already know some keywords. Even if you have a job description from an advertisement for a job, it's likely that you know some keywords, because it's likely that they appear right there.

It's true: the best way to identify keywords is to look closely at a job description. You can almost bet that some of the words and phrases from the job description will be the keywords that are used to search a database to find qualified applicants. If you don't have a specific job description, you need to know enough about the occupation that interests you so that you can make an educated guess about the keywords that will be used in the search.

Because nearly every word or phrase in a job description is a potential keyword, you need to pay very close attention to the wording of job descriptions (yes, even those that appear in classified ads). To maximize your chances of being selected by the computer search, you need to include those words and phrases in your resume or application EXACTLY AS THEY APPEAR IN THE DESCRIPTION. If an ad uses the phrase "three years of experience," then your resume should use the same phrase. If a job description notes that a "B.S. Degree in Biology" is required, your resume should contain the same phrase.

Keywords are a key to success these days. As you have seen in the preceding chapters (if you haven't read them, you probably should), there is a strong possibility that when you apply for a job, your resume or application will be entered into an electronic database. You don't have any control over that. If the company or recruitment firm that lists the job uses a computer to track its applicants, chances are great that your resume will be put into it.

The one thing over which you do have some control is how your resume will get out of the computer. The way you want it to emerge is as a "hit" or "match" in a search. This means that your qualifications match the qualifications required for a job.

When your resume has been selected, it is usually printed out and sent to a person who is directly involved in the hiring process (or transmitted electronically to that person). That's your goal. You want your resume to get out of the computer and onto the desk of a person who can hire you! Using keywords in your resume can improve the odds of getting selected in the computerized search. Once you know that fact, you understand why you need to include keywords in your resume.

To help you get the idea of how to extract keywords from job descriptions, included below is a section that contains actual job listings followed by suggestions for how parts of a resume might be worded in response. These are only suggestions, but they should provide you with clues that can help you with your own resume.

Following that section is a section where you can practice extracting keywords from job descriptions in your own field. Space is included so that you can enter descriptions that you have identified on your own. Additional space is provided for you to note how you might respond in your resume. This means that you are developing your own, personalized list of keywords! It may seem easy to you, but it's an essential part of resume writing today. If you remember to use the keyword approach in every resume you produce, you will have a definite advantage over other applicants who have never heard of keywords.

Take a few minutes right now to look through the section below. Then take some time to collect job descriptions that look interesting to you, from jobs you want to apply for or from jobs that you have recently applied for. It's worth the time. Once you're in the habit of customizing your resume with keywords, you will wonder why you haven't done it sooner. It makes sense. And it offers a terrific "payoff" to.

SAMPLE JOB DESCRIPTIONS

CUSTOMER SERVICE REPRESENTATIVE

Primary duties include handling customer billing inquiries, answering phones, responding to customer letters, computing credit adjustments, producing reports, and handling special projects as assigned. Qualified candidates will have a strong desire to serve customers and resolve conflicts, excellent written and oral communication skills, and be personable self-starters who can work independently. Previous customer service is desirable.

This is a typical job description for a kind of job that is widely advertised. This particular description was placed in a major metropolitan newspaper by a large consumer-products corporation. The company was probably flooded with resumes in response to their ad. It is very likely that someone in the human relations department that received those resumes looked at each of them briefly, to see if the minimum qualifications had been met, and then scanned them into a computerized applicant tracking system.

When it was time to examine the pool of applicants, a search was conducted—by entering "keywords" into the computer and looking at the names and resumes that were retrieved. Because those resumes with the most "hits"—the most matches with the keywords used in the search—were probably the first resumes to be retrieved, the applicants who used those same keywords in their resumes were probably at the top of the list of candidates.

Take a look at the ad above. If you had the job of conducting the computerized search, which words and phrases would you pick out as "keywords" to use in that search? First, of course, you would put in the job title itself to see if candidates had held a job with the same title: "Customer Service Representative." Second, you would probably enter the phrase "customer service" or maybe "customer service experience." Then you would just start entering phrases and words from the ad itself (since the ad was presumably taken directly from the job description): billing inquiries, answering phones (or just "phone" or "telephone"), credit adjustments, reports, special projects, resolve conflicts (or "conflict resolution"), communication skills, writing skills, self-starter, personable, independent.

Note how brief the keywords are. Note, too, that they can be from all parts of the ad (and from all parts of a resume). They refer to skills, qualifications, and experiences. They could easily include words and phrases from other parts of a resume, including education and accomplishments, to name just two. It's easy to see how the job description or the advertisement provides within it the basis of the keywords search.

After they have identified the words and phrases that are likely to be used as keywords, how can applicants for this job be sure that the keywords appear in their resumes? There are several ways, and each of them is easy to follow. First, a candidate could include a section at the top of a resume (right under the name and address) with a heading of "Profile" or "Summary" or "Qualifications." For this job, it might be worded like this:

Experienced customer service representative, with experience in billing inquiries, answering phones, credit adjustments, writing reports, and completing special projects. Possess excellent communications skills, both oral and written. A self-starter, who can work independently. Personable, with strong desire to serve customers and resolve conflicts.

With an introductory section like that, this would be a resume that would be noticed! Both computers and humans would pay attention. Of course, the rest of the resume would have to document exactly how those qualifications were obtained, and that leads to the second way that keywords can be incorporated into resumes. They can be added to the sections where they fit best.

Even without an introductory section, you can see that it would be easy to include keywords for this job in several sections of a resume, like experience, skills, personal qualifications, and others.

Here is another example, also taken from the "help wanted" section of a newspaper:

PUBLIC RELATIONS ASSOCIATE

Responsibilities include proposal preparation, donor research, fund raising, marketing, database management, news releases, newsletter, and gala events. Need superior communication skills, computer experience (PC, Windows, WordPerfect, Lotus preferred), ability to work closely with others, plan projects, and raise money. BA/BS degree, related work experience. High energy a plus.

In this ad, almost every word or phrase could be a keyword! If you were applying for this position, you would want to try to work into your resume nearly everything that appears in the ad. And it wouldn't be hard to do either. If you had already prepared a resume, you could add a "summary" section that utilized the keywords that the ad suggests or you could go through the resume to see exactly where it would be most appropriate to add the keywords.

THE "KEYWORDS WORKSHEET"

You won't always have such clear job descriptions or such well-worded advertisements to respond to when you are preparing a resume. That's exactly why you need to know what your future employers are most likely to want from a person in your position. In other words, you need your own personal list of keywords.

In the spaces below, write down the words and phrases that you think are most likely to be used by either humans or computers as they review your resume. (This task is made easier if you have some advertisements or job descriptions for the kinds of jobs you hope to get. If you have some, spread them out around you as you complete the following sections.) If you are planning to apply for more than one type of job, photocopy these sheets or simply write on additional pieces of paper.

JOB TITLE _____

SKILLS KEYWORDS_____

_____

_____

QUALIFICATIONS KEYWORDS_____

_____

_____

EXPERIENCE KEYWORDS_____

_____

_____

EDUCATION KEYWORDS _____

_____

_____

TECHNICAL KEYWORDS _____

_____

_____

MISCELLANEOUS KEYWORDS _____

_____

Congratulations! You are ready to start writing your resume! The following chapters will take you step-by-step through the process of developing the resume that is right for you. You will want to refer back to your personal list of keywords frequently as you develop your resume.

Including keywords is a simple thing to do, and it will give you an advantage in today's job market, where computers are playing an increasingly important role. Learning to "think like a computer" is a valuable skill in writing a resume these days. And you have a head start! But don't stop here. Move on to the next chapter and see how easy it is to start writing a terrific resume.

CHAPTER 5

BUILDING A RESUME

START WITH SKILLS

This book is designed to take you step by step through the entire process of constructing your own resume. The approach is simple and straightforward. By using the worksheets in the following chapters, you will be creating sections of your resume. At the end of the worksheet chapters, you will learn how to assemble these sections into the perfect resume for you. In fact, you will learn how to assemble different resumes for different purposes—different jobs for example. This "building block" approach will provide you with the pieces you need to construct a resume every time you need one.

In today's competition for jobs, it is essential that you submit the best resume you can every time you apply for a job. And that is just what this book can help you do. The best news of all, though, is that the process is easy and painless.

Just follow the directions, fill out the worksheets, and your resume will be ready to put together! And it will be ready to send by mail, by fax, or by "electronic mail." (If you have borrowed this book from a library or from a friend, you should photocopy the worksheets and write on the copies. Better yet, buy a copy of the book for yourself and then you can write in it as much as you want to!)

YOUR PERSONAL SKILLS

The logical place to begin work on your resume is by describing yourself. This doesn't mean a long introduction that describes your life. Your biography might interest members of your family (some of them anyway) but it won't hold the attention of most employers. Employers want to know what you have to offer. When you are applying for a job, it will pay you to "think like an employer." If you were doing the hiring, what would you be looking for in a prospective employee?

When you think about it, probably the first question you would ask is "What can this person do for me?" And that is exactly the question that your resume must answer. The answer needs to be easy to find because employers don't spend much time looking over an individual resume. (Estimates of the exact amount of time employers do spend vary, but it's safe to say that your resume is given less than one minute to answer this all-important question.)

In the past, resumes reported only on-the-job experience. This approach helped those people who had been employed already and who were planning to take another step on the same career path. Everybody else—those looking for a job for the first time, those who were reentering the workforce, those who were trying to change careers, those trying to leap up the corporate ladder without climbing it rung by rung, and many others—was hurt by this work-experience approach to resumes.

From the point of view of employers, the jobs-only emphasis wasn't tremendously useful either. What employers learned from traditional resumes was only what an applicant *had done in the past* and not what that applicant *could do in the future*. This really didn't help employers all that much since what they really want to know is: "What can this person do for me from this day forward?" and not "What did this person do before?"

Employers have always known that some of their best employees have been people whose past experiences didn't lead them very directly to their current positions. But they have also been afraid to take chances in hiring new employees who haven't already performed exactly the same job somewhere else. It's hard to predict which employees can take on new responsibilities successfully. Rather than take a chance, most employers have given jobs to people who have done similar work before.

Employers know that there are other people out in the job market who could do the job too—maybe could do

an even better job—but they don't know how to identify them. By including your personal skills on your resume, you are providing a way for employers to spot your talents, even if your work background doesn't appear to lead directly to the job you want next.

IDENTIFYING YOUR SKILLS

You may not know it right now, but you have a unique set of skills. You have acquired your skills in every activity in which you have ever participated. They haven't come only from your past jobs (although you may have plenty of job skills as well). You have collected them in volunteer work, in working at home, in being a student, in your hobbies and in your extracurricular activities.

Skills are often *transferable* from one occupation to another. For example, teachers frequently say to career counselors: "I'm a teacher. What skills do I have besides teaching?" The answer is: "You have a lot!" And they do. Teachers have skills like time planning, supervising and motivating individuals and groups, setting goals, evaluating results, public speaking, and many others. So do you.

The skills worksheets that follow are designed to help you identify your particular skills. They begin by asking you to list a specific activity which has been significant to you. You can start with your most recent job or you can start with any other role that has been important for you. If you really can't think of a place to start, simply list the activity that takes up most of your time each day (besides sleeping!).

You will be asked to describe the activity. Write this description in the way you might say it out loud to an employer if you were asked in an interview "Tell me a little bit about that." It doesn't have to be polished or precise right now because you will have an opportunity to rewrite it again.

NAMING YOUR SKILLS

The next step on the worksheets that follow is to put a name to the skills you used or learned in the activity you selected. You will be surprised at how many you can name. Some of the skills you list are skills that you already had when you began the activity. You may have learned these in school, from a previous job, from your parents, or just from living. All of these "count" here. All are important.

If you find yourself listing skills that you don't want to use on a job (or skills you don't want anyone to know you have), drop these and concentrate on those that you would be comfortable discussing with an employer. For example, if one of your activities has been to raise a child from infancy to kindergarten, you might have acquired undeniable skills in changing diapers. However, if you are not looking for a job in child care, this is a skill that won't be much in demand. Focus instead on the time planning, household

management, and related skills that you had to employ in child rearing.

Following the worksheets there is a sample list of skills you can refer to after you make your own list, in case you forgot to include some of the skills you used or learned.

There are four skills worksheets included. You can complete fewer than four or do more if you want (photocopy the worksheets or use your own sheets of paper if you want to analyze more than four activities).

THE SKILLS SUMMARY

After you have identified skills for your activities, you will be ready to fill out the "Skills Summary" worksheet. Here you will be asked to look over the skills that you recorded for each activity and to take a look at the sample list too. From these, you will select the personal skills that you would like a prospective employer to see. You may be surprised to discover how many of your skills really are of interest to employers. This is just the kind of information they want to know, but have never been able to discover on resumes in the past.

Don't worry now about how you will use these skills in your resume. That will become clear later. For now, fill out the worksheets and the skills summary and congratulate yourself on getting started on your resume.

SKILLS WORKSHEET

Activity (This can be a job, a volunteer activity, a hobby, etc.)

_____

_____

Description of the activity (Briefly describe what you did.)

_____

_____

_____

_____

_____

Skills you used or learned in the activity _____

_____

_____

_____

_____

_____

(Refer to the sample list of skills after you have made your own and add any from the list that you haven't included already.)

SKILLS WORKSHEET

Activity (This can be a job, a volunteer activity, a hobby, etc.)

_____

_____

Description of the activity (Briefly describe what you did.)

_____

_____

_____

_____

_____

Skills you used or learned in the activity _____

_____

_____

_____

_____

_____

(Refer to the sample list of skills after you have made your own and add any from the list that you haven't included already.)

SKILLS WORKSHEET

Activity (This can be a job, a volunteer activity, a hobby, etc.)

_____
_____

Description of the activity (Briefly describe what you did.)

_____
_____
_____
_____
_____

Skills you used or learned in the activity _____
_____
_____
_____
_____
_____

(Refer to the sample list of skills after you have made your own and add any from the list that you haven't included already.)

SKILLS WORKSHEET

Activity (This can be a job, a volunteer activity, a hobby, etc.)

_____
_____

Description of the activity (Briefly describe what you did.)

_____
_____
_____
_____
_____

Skills you used or learned in the activity _____
_____
_____
_____
_____
_____

(Refer to the sample list of skills after you have made your own and add any from the list that you haven't included already.)

SKILLS SUMMARY

From the skills you identified on the skills worksheets and from the sample list of skills, note below those skills that you would like a prospective employer to know about you. For each skill that you include, ask yourself one question: Will I be comfortable talking with a future employer about this? If the answer is no, drop it from your list of skills. If you're not sure, leave it on your list for now.

1. _____

2. _____

3. _____

4. _____

5. _____

6. _____

7. _____

8. _____

9. _____

10. _____

Congratulations! You have completed the first step in creating your own resume! Don't stop here, though. The next chapter is even easier than this one.

SAMPLE LIST OF SKILLS

Every activity requires skills. Every task you perform demands some kind of skill, whether the task is part of a job, a hobby, a volunteer position, or working around your house or apartment. Sometimes it is hard to identify the skills you are using because they seem like "second nature" or like they are "automatic." This sample list is here to stimulate your thinking about skills. It certainly isn't comprehensive, but it can trigger your thoughts as you analyze your activities. Refer to this list as you complete the Skills Worksheets and the Skills Summary.

Instructing	Counseling
Selling	Analyzing
Coordinating	Supervising
Planning	Leading
Communicating	Persuading
Coaching	Teaching
Finding solutions	Keeping records
Mediating	Explaining
Innovating	Making decisions
Solving problems	Resolving conflicts
Motivating	Writing
Creating	Bookkeeping
Attending to details	Budgeting
Tracking progress	Managing time
Increasing profit	Increasing productivity
Stimulating sales	Stimulating growth

SAMPLE LIST OF SKILLS

Operating (equipment)	Using computers
Overseeing projects	Using software packages
Managing staff	Negotiating
Reporting	Programming
Conceiving	Hiring
Designing	Editing
Producing	Translating
Building	Repairing
Monitoring	Interviewing
Organizing	Reorganizing
Evaluating	Recommending
Training	Investigating
Researching	Increasing efficiency

CHAPTER 6

PERSONAL QUALIFICATIONS

WHO ARE YOU?

"Personal qualifications" are just as important as skills, but (just like skills) they usually don't appear on resumes. That's too bad, because including these on a resume is one of the best ways to "come alive" for an employer. You have already identified the "keywords" of the job you want in a previous chapter. (If you haven't, you might want to do that before you develop a list of your personal qualifications.) To come up with your list of keywords you probably looked at job descriptions of jobs that interest you. In those descriptions you might have noticed that there were words and phrases that weren't exactly "job related." The ads might have said things like "well organized," or "quick learner," or "works well under pressure." All of these words are "personal qualifications."

People often refer to their qualifications as "aspects of my personality." You might say: "That's just who I am." Well, who are you? That's what you need to put down on paper under the heading of personal qualifications. Your assignment in this chapter is to describe your personality. It might help you to view this assignment as if you were someone else—maybe your best friend—describing you. What would that person say are the best aspects of your personality?

Personal qualifications are sometimes called "traits" or "qualities." They are usually best described with short phrases, like: calm under pressure; good with my hands; can talk to just about anybody; easy to get along with; able to do many things at once, etc. Don't think of these only as job related. You are trying to describe yourself to someone who has never met you. You're creating a "word picture" of yourself.

Of course, you want to emphasize the positive aspects of your personality. This is not the place to note for example: "I'm a real hothead" or "I drive people nuts with my constant talking." These may be aspects of your personality, but they're not what we're looking for here!

If you find it difficult to describe your personal qualifications, even after you have tried to look at yourself as your best friend might look at you, it's time to ask your best friend for help. Ask that friend (better yet, ask two or three) to describe your best qualities. Take notes while your friend is talking and then transfer your notes to the worksheet. (After all, what are friends for if not to tell you what they think is best about you?)

There is a list of sample personal qualifications right after the worksheet, in case you want to add to your list. But don't go right to this sample list. You (and your best friend) can describe you much better than the list can.

Personal qualifications, along with skills, are the "missing links" in resumes. These are the just the kinds of things that employers want to know about their prospective employees, but they are rarely found on resumes.

Employers often report that they want to know "What sort of person is this?" or "What is this person really like?" What they are asking, in fact, is "What personal qualifications does this person have?"

If you read the chapter on "keywords," you noticed how many "personal qualifications" were included in the sample job descriptions that appeared there. And if you looked through job advertisements before you completed the "Keywords Worksheet," you probably saw the same thing. Employers may not know it, but they ask frequently about personal qualifications.

If you include personal qualifications on your resume, you will answer some of the first (and most important) questions that employers ask as they are studying resumes and trying to figure out which candidates to call in for interviews. By incorporating your personal qualifications, you are speaking directly to employers about what is really on their minds—and you are increasing your chances of being asked to come in for an interview!

PERSONAL QUALIFICATIONS WORKSHEET

What are your best personal qualities? (Briefly describe them with a word or a phrase.)

1._____

2._____

3._____

4._____

5._____

6._____

7._____

8._____

9._____

10._____

After you have made your list, refer to the sample list that begins on the page after next and add any other qualifications that you feel you have. Then move immediately to the Job Qualifications Worksheet on the following page.

JOB QUALIFICATIONS WORKSHEET

After you have described your personal qualifications on the preceding worksheet, and after you have looked over the sample list, take a minute to determine which of your qualifications are likely to interest an employer. (There should be at least two or three, and perhaps many more.) On this worksheet, list these as "job qualifications," just the way you might include them on your resume.

1._____

2._____

3._____

4._____

5._____

6._____

7._____

8._____

9._____

10._____

Congratulations! You have completed another step in creating your own best resume (and you are probably learning more about what you have to offer to employers too). Now it's time to move on to the next section.

PERSONAL QUALIFICATIONS

The descriptive words below are only a sample of the kinds of words you might use to describe yourself. There are many other possible personal qualifications. Use the list to stimulate your own thoughts about your best qualities. Refer to it when you are filling out your Personal Qualifications Worksheet and your Job Qualifications Worksheet.

Reliable	Dependable
Well-organized	Quick learner
Self-motivated	Self-starter
Imaginative	Bright
Smart	Intelligent
Thorough	Conscientious
Persuasive	Diplomatic
Friendly	Outgoing
Loyal	Persistent
Practical	Problem-solver
Active	Calm
Trustworthy	Inquisitive
Dedicated	Giving
Methodical	Productive
Creative	Ingenious
Inventive	Prolific
Clever	Original
Systematic	Businesslike

Professional	Honest
Unique	Skilled
Talented	Adept
Able	Competent
Efficient	Proficient
Exceptional	Congenial
Devoted	Energetic
Aggressive	Assertive
Genial	Gregarious
Truthful	Composed
Patient	Tenacious
Poised	Even-tempered
Astute	Incisive
Perceptive	Rational
Curious	Discerning
Sensible	Thoughtful
Precise	Flexible
Insightful	Caring
Versatile	Responsible
Analytic	Organized

CHAPTER 7

EXPERIENCE

WRITING ABOUT YOUR "WORK"

In the past, resumes included mostly descriptions of current and previous jobs. As the preceding chapters have made clear, resumes have changed. The ideal resume today tries to communicate much more about the "whole person." Even so, "work experience" remains an essential part of any resume. Obviously employers want to know the kinds of jobs that you have held in the past, what your responsibilities were in those jobs, and what you achieved or accomplished in each. It is your responsibility in writing your resume to discuss your experience. Fortunately the manner in which you present the information is entirely up to you. If you look through the sample resumes at the back of this book you will see a surprising variety in how "work experience" is presented.

"Work experience" has quotation marks around it because it actually refers to more than work. In this section, you will focus on your experiences that are "work-like," whether or not you actually got paid or had a formal job. You might want to use the experiences that gave you some of the "personal skills" you have already recorded—the experiences that we called "activities" in the chapter where you analyzed your personal skills. If there are other experiences that you hope to include on your resume, you should complete a Work Experience Worksheet for each experience.

HOW TO USE THE "WORK EXPERIENCE" WORKSHEETS

Completing the "Work Experience" Worksheets is a four-stage process. First you will describe the experience; second, you will add "action words"; third, you will put in "facts and figures"; and fourth, you will include "keywords" wherever you can. With each "Work Experience" Worksheet you complete, you will have added another "building block" for constructing your resume.

If you have held jobs, you will probably want to use those jobs—and job titles—on your "Work Experience" Worksheets. If you have not worked (or haven't worked in the last ten years or more), you will want to use the kind of experience you used on your Skills Worksheet: a volunteer or unpaid position, a part-time job, a summer job, an internship or "co-op" position, a job in the home, etc.

In fact, if you have held a responsible position as a volunteer, you may want to add this to your list of experiences even if you have also been employed at a full-time job as well. Employers like to know what people do *outside* their jobs; if you have been able to hold a significant volunteer position, it says something positive about you. If you decide to include unpaid work on your resume, in addition to paid experience, simply fill out a Work Experience Worksheet for each of these unpaid experiences.

The "Work Experience" Worksheets are easy to use. First, complete the top of the form. Start with your present job or position on the first worksheet and then work backwards chronologically through your previous jobs, activities, or unpaid positions. List the main responsibilities of your position next to the numbers. Begin with your most important responsibility next to number one and work down in priority if you can. (If you can't put your responsibilities into a ranked order very easily, don't worry about it. Any order is fine for now.)

"ACTION WORDS"

Once you have recorded the key tasks of the position, use the next section of the form to re-word these tasks so that they include *action words*. These are essential to the success of your resume. Ideally, the descriptions of your positions will consist of short phrases that each begin with an action word. There is a list of sample action words at the end of the "Work Experience" Worksheets. You can take words from this list or use your own words. You may even want to look through the sample resumes at the back of the book to see how "action words" look in action in finished re-

sumes. The secrets here are to keep the phrases brief and the first words "strong."

For example, you might have said in the first section of the worksheet: "As the assistant to the purchasing manager, I make sure that bid forms go out to possible vendors and then I record the bids when they come back in. I have an assistant who takes care of the filing and the mailing." Now you are going to transform those statements by shortening them and using action words. Your new description might come out like this: "Coordinate bid process. Identify vendors. Send bid forms. Track responses. Supervise filing and mailing staff."

You can do this for any responsibilities and for any jobs. It's not hard to do. Just use the action words list and cut out any unnecessary words. This has two important results. First, it makes your descriptions easy for prospective employers to read and to understand. Second, it commands attention. This is a powerful way to communicate with potential employers.

"FACTS AND FIGURES"

The next step in perfecting the descriptions of your "work experience" is to add "facts and figures." This is the way you make your job or activity as concrete as possible. The questions to answer here are "How many?" "How much time?" "For whom?" "With what results?" There may be others that apply to your position. In the example we used above, we might add: "Contact approximately 250 vendors a year. Process bids in excess of $500,000 a year. File more than 2000 pages per year. Handle more than 30 phone calls a day for the purchasing department."

Again, you can do this for any job or activity, paid or unpaid. It requires some estimating on your part, but no one knows your responsibilities better than you do. You will probably be surprised at the numbers you can add here.

These "facts and figures" are vital in a resume. They really bring your job to life. And they make a positive impression on employers. They add substance to your experience and to your resume. This is an extremely useful addition to your resume and it is a step that is often forgotten by resume writers. It is included as a separate step here so that you won't forget it.

"KEYWORDS"

You already know how important "keywords" are for resumes today. Because the chances are good that your resume will be electronically "scanned" and "searched," it is essential that keywords—those words and phrases that are likely to be part of the electronic search—show up on your resume. If you have completed the worksheet in the "keywords" chapter of this book, you have a good idea of the exact words and phrases that may be used in a computerized search of your resume. (If you haven't completed the

worksheets in that chapter, now is a good time to go back and fill them out. It takes a little time, but it is worth the effort.)

The final task of the Work Experience Worksheet is add the essential "experience" keywords from your own worksheet in the "keywords" chapter. There are probably several specific words and phrases that you have identified. This is the place to make sure that the keywords which relate to experience are included.

Take a minute and go back to your Keywords Worksheet. Look over the list you generated. Then come back to the Work Experience Worksheet and make sure that all of the relevant keywords appear, exactly as you want to phrase them. It is perfectly OK to include the same keywords more than once. Just make sure they are included!

The four-part process you will use to fill out the Work Experience Worksheets is crucial for your resume. Be sure to finish all four steps for each "experience." There are five worksheets included in this chapter. If you need more than five, photocopy the worksheet or use separate sheets of paper and follow the same process.

WORK EXPERIENCE WORKSHEET

Job title (or position held): _____

Employer (company, agency, etc.) _____

Dates From_____(month/year) To _____ (month/year)

Briefly describe your employer _____

_____

Responsibilities. Describe what you did in this job or activity.
1.

2.

3.

Add "action words." Restate each of the responsibilities above but make each statement brief and begin each with an action word (see the list of "action words" that follows).
1.

2.

3.

Add "facts and figures." Be as specific as you can (numbers, dollars, etc.).
1.

2.

3.

Add "keywords." Include your own keywords. Be sure that your wording is precise.
1.

2.

3.

Congratulations on completing the Work Experience Worksheets. These are vital "building blocks" for your resume.

WORK EXPERIENCE WORKSHEET

Job title (or position held): _____

Employer (company, agency, etc.) _____

Dates From_____(month/year) To _____ (month/year)

Briefly describe your employer _____

_____

Responsibilities. Describe what you did in this job or activity.

1.

2.

3.

Add "action words." Restate each of the responsibilities above but make each statement brief and begin each with an action word (see the list of "action words" that follows).

1.

2.

3.

Add "facts and figures." Be as specific as you can (numbers, dollars, etc.).

1.

2.

3.

Add "keywords." Include your own keywords. Be sure that your wording is precise.

1.

2.

3.

Congratulations on completing the Work Experience Worksheets. These are vital "building blocks" for your resume.

WORK EXPERIENCE WORKSHEET

Job title (or position held): _____

Employer (company, agency, etc.) _____

Dates From_____(month/year) To _____ (month/year)

Briefly describe your employer _____

_____

Responsibilities. Describe what you did in this job or activity.
1.

2.

3.

Add "action words." Restate each of the responsibilities above but make each statement brief and begin each with an action word (see the list of "action words" that follows).
1.

2.

3.

Add "facts and figures." Be as specific as you can (numbers, dollars, etc.).
1.

2.

3.

Add "keywords." Include your own keywords. Be sure that your wording is precise.
1.

2.

3.

Congratulations on completing the Work Experience Worksheets. These are vital "building blocks" for your resume.

WORK EXPERIENCE WORKSHEET

Job title (or position held): _____

Employer (company, agency, etc.) _____

Dates From_____(month/year) To _____ (month/year)

Briefly describe your employer _____

_____

Responsibilities. Describe what you did in this job or activity.
1.

2.

3.

Add "action words." Restate each of the responsibilities above but make each statement brief and begin each with an action word (see the list of "action words" that follows).
1.

2.

3.

Add "facts and figures." Be as specific as you can (numbers, dollars, etc.).
1.

2.

3.

Add "keywords." Include your own keywords. Be sure that your wording is precise.
1.

2.

3.

Congratulations on completing the Work Experience Worksheets. These are vital "building blocks" for your resume.

WORK EXPERIENCE WORKSHEET

Job title (or position held): _____

Employer (company, agency, etc.) _____

Dates From_____(month/year) To _____ (month/year)

Briefly describe your employer _____

_____

Responsibilities. Describe what you did in this job or activity.
1.

2.

3.

Add "action words." Restate each of the responsibilities above but make each statement brief and begin each with an action word (see the list of "action words" that follows).
1.

2.

3.

Add "facts and figures." Be as specific as you can (numbers, dollars, etc.).
1.

2.

3.

Add "keywords." Include your own keywords. Be sure that your wording is precise.
1.

2.

3.

Congratulations on completing the Work Experience Worksheets. These are vital "building blocks" for your resume.

To communicate quickly and powerfully with prospective employers, use "action" words wherever you can on your resume (and in your cover letter too). This list will provide you with suggestions but it should not confine you. If you have a better word, use it.

"Action words" usually begin short sentences or phrases, like "Coordinated fund-raising campaign," or "Implemented new office procedures," or "Trained new sales force." Take a look at the sample resumes at the back of the book to see how other job seekers have used "action words" in their resumes.

The list is placed here to help you add "action words" to your "work experience," accomplishments, and job skills worksheets, but use them wherever you think they are effective.

Developed	Initiated
Coordinated	Controlled
Advised	Authored
Performed	Implemented
Recommended	Designed
Maintained	Analyzed
Operated	Explained
Reviewed	Monitored
Suggested	Compiled
Generated	Adjusted
Produced	Revised
Created	Adapted
Supervised	Instructed
Planned	Enhanced
Built	Modified

Wrote	Reported
Determined	Debugged
Organized	Augmented
Conceived	Acquired
Purchased	Executed
Managed	Proposed
Assisted	Negotiated
Evaluated	Corresponded
Trained	Streamlined
Documented	Provided
Persuaded	Promoted
Improved	Examined
Simplified	Invented
Engineered	Arranged
Contacted	Packaged
Recognized	Programmed
Collected	Placed
Prepared	Saved
Merged	Investigated
Taught	Coached
Researched	Discovered
Counseled	Assembled
Constructed	Estimated

Installed	Repaired
Screened	Dispatched
Inspected	Audited
Budgeted	Cultivated
Tested	Appraised
Manufactured	Elicited
Lectured	Lobbied
Advertised	Interviewed
Hired	Fired
Logged	Catalogued
Copyrighted	Patented
Inventoried	Posted
Edited	Balanced
Steered	Vended
Translated	Transcribed
Rescued	Displayed
Took part in	Closed (a deal)
Was in charge of	Was responsible for
Accomplished	Presented
Completed	Reorganized
Identified	Delivered
Restored	Instituted
Diagnosed	Sold

Made	Guided
Founded	Approved
Administered	Replaced
Increased	Established
Expanded	Calculated
Directed	Supplied
Produced	Headed
Interpreted	Represented
Scheduled	Distributed
Achieved	Conducted
Obtained	Selected
Referred	Formulated
Enlarged	Motivated
Devised	Solved
Studied	Ordered
Led	Consolidated
Eliminated	Decreased
Designated	Reduced
Processed	Composed
Served	Disproved
Detected	Won

CHAPTER 8

ACCOMPLISHMENTS

WRITING ABOUT YOUR ACHIEVEMENTS

In every job or position you have had, whether it was paid or unpaid, you have had "accomplishments." You have achieved something. You might have had large-scale accomplishments—like securing a new contract worth a million dollars to your company or starting up a new branch office by yourself—or your accomplishments may have been on a smaller scale—like reorganizing a filing system or just getting everything done on time. This is exactly the place to note these accomplishments.

"Why is it important to list my accomplishments?" you may be asking. The answer is that they show initiative on your part and an awareness of the needs of your employer too. They demonstrate tangibly the *contributions* you have made in the past and they suggest the kinds of contributions that you could make in the future. This is exactly the kind of information that employers want but rarely find on resumes. It helps them to see what you might be able to do for them if they hired you.

The format of the Accomplishment Worksheet is very similar to that of the Work Experience Worksheets you completed in the previous chapter. Staying with the example that was used there, the assistant to the purchasing manager might fill out the Accomplishments Worksheet like this: "Streamlined purchasing process, saving the company time and paper. Started first computerized tracking process, making it possible to check the status of any vendor or bid. Found approximately 45 new vendors, resulting in savings of more than $25,000 in first year on the job."

As you can see, "action words," "facts and figures," and "keywords" are as important on the Accomplishments Worksheet as they were on the Work Experience Worksheets. The sheets are set up in the same way and use the same four-step process. First, note your accomplishments. Second, add action words. (Refer to the list that precedes this chapter if you need suggestions.) Third, add facts and figures. Fourth, check to see if you can include keywords.

This isn't a time to be bashful. Everyone, in every position, has had accomplishments. If you genuinely cannot think of your accomplishments, take a look at any evaluation forms you or your supervisor might have filled out or ask a co-worker to suggest some possibilities to you.

ACCOMPLISHMENTS WORKSHEET

Use the same experiences for your Accomplishments Worksheets that you used on your Work Experience Worksheets. Remember that these can be paid or unpaid jobs, part-time jobs, summer jobs, volunteer activities, internships, jobs in the home, etc. The focus here is on what you have <u>achieved</u>. Remember to be as specific as possible.

Job title (or position held): _____

Accomplishments

1.

2.

3.

Add "action words." Rewrite the statements above so that each begins with an action word. Refer to the list of action words at the end of the preceding chapter if you need help.

1.

2.

3.

Add "facts and figures." If you haven't included the specifics of your accomplishments, do it now. Rewrite each statement so that it includes numbers, dollars, etc.

1.

2.

3.

Add "keywords." Take a look at your list of keywords and see if any can be added to your accomplishments. The wording below should be written exactly as you want each accomplishment to appear in your resume. This is your "final draft."

1.

2.

3.

ACCOMPLISHMENTS WORKSHEET

Use the same experiences for your Accomplishments Worksheets that you used on your Work Experience Worksheets. Remember that these can be paid or unpaid jobs, part-time jobs, summer jobs, volunteer activities, internships, jobs in the home, etc. The focus here is on what you have <u>achieved</u>. Remember to be as specific as possible.

Job title (or position held): _____

Accomplishments

1.

2.

3.

Add "action words." Rewrite the statements above so that each begins with an action word. Refer to the list of action words at the end of the preceding chapter if you need help.

1.

2.

3.

Add "facts and figures." If you haven't included the specifics of your accomplishments, do it now. Rewrite each statement so that it includes numbers, dollars, etc.

1.

2.

3.

Add "keywords." Take a look at your list of keywords and see if any can be added to your accomplishments. The wording below should be written exactly as you want each accomplishment to appear in your resume. This is your "final draft."

1.

2.

3.

ACCOMPLISHMENTS WORKSHEET

Use the same experiences for your Accomplishments Worksheets that you used on your Work Experience Worksheets. Remember that these can be paid or unpaid jobs, part-time jobs, summer jobs, volunteer activities, internships, jobs in the home, etc. The focus here is on what you have <u>achieved</u>. Remember to be as specific as possible.

Job title (or position held): _____

Accomplishments

1.

2.

3.

Add "action words." Rewrite the statements above so that each begins with an action word. Refer to the list of action words at the end of the preceding chapter if you need help.

1.

2.

3.

Add "facts and figures." If you haven't included the specifics of your accomplishments, do it now. Rewrite each statement so that it includes numbers, dollars, etc.

1.

2.

3.

Add "keywords." Take a look at your list of keywords and see if any can be added to your accomplishments. The wording below should be written exactly as you want each accomplishment to appear in your resume. This is your "final draft."

1.

2.

3.

ACCOMPLISHMENTS WORKSHEET

Use the same experiences for your Accomplishments Worksheets that you used on your Work Experience Worksheets. Remember that these can be paid or unpaid jobs, part-time jobs, summer jobs, volunteer activities, internships, jobs in the home, etc. The focus here is on what you have <u>achieved</u>. Remember to be as specific as possible.

Job title (or position held): _____

Accomplishments

1.

2.

3.

Add "action words." Rewrite the statements above so that each begins with an action word. Refer to the list of action words at the end of the preceding chapter if you need help.

1.

2.

3.

Add "facts and figures." If you haven't included the specifics of your accomplishments, do it now. Rewrite each statement so that it includes numbers, dollars, etc.

1.

2.

3.

Add "keywords." Take a look at your list of keywords and see if any can be added to your accomplishments. The wording below should be written exactly as you want each accomplishment to appear in your resume. This is your "final draft."

1.

2.

3.

ACCOMPLISHMENTS WORKSHEET

Use the same experiences for your Accomplishments Worksheets that you used on your Work Experience Worksheets. Remember that these can be paid or unpaid jobs, part-time jobs, summer jobs, volunteer activities, internships, jobs in the home, etc. The focus here is on what you have <u>achieved</u>. Remember to be as specific as possible.

Job title (or position held): _____

Accomplishments

1.

2.

3.

Add "action words." Rewrite the statements above so that each begins with an action word. Refer to the list of action words at the end of the preceding chapter if you need help.

1.

2.

3.

Add "facts and figures." If you haven't included the specifics of your accomplishments, do it now. Rewrite each statement so that it includes numbers, dollars, etc.

1.

2.

3.

Add "keywords." Take a look at your list of keywords and see if any can be added to your accomplishments. The wording below should be written exactly as you want each accomplishment to appear in your resume. This is your "final draft."

1.

2.

3.

CHAPTER 9

JOB SKILLS

WRITING ABOUT WORK-RELATED SKILLS

Everyone who has ever worked has "job skills." Even if you haven't held a paying job, you have "job skills." These are any skills that you have had to use to get your job or tasks or assignments done. In completing the Job Skills Worksheets, it is useful to "think like an employer" and identify skills that might be needed in the kinds of jobs you want. Employers, as you would guess, are keenly interested in the job-related skills that you have acquired in the past because you bring all of these skills with you into a new job.

On the Job Skills Worksheets that follow, you can note any skills that you have used in previous jobs or activities, like the kinds of equipment you know how to operate or the computers and software packages you know how to use. Include skills here like your proficiency in speaking or writing languages other than English, as well as skills that are specific to your occupation. Once again, you will be asked to use action words, make your skills as "fact filled" as possible, and include any relevant keywords.

The purchasing assistant whom we have been using as an example in previous chapters might record job skills like these: "Proficient in use of WordPerfect and Xywrite word processing software. Type 75 words per minute. Regularly use Lotus 1-2-3 spreadsheet software. Speak conversational Spanish. Often draft letters for supervisor." These are the kinds of skills you have too—and this is the spot to include them. If you can't think of the kinds of job skills you have, take a look at your job description (if you have one), your on-the-job evaluations by your supervisor, or ask a colleague. Looking through the resumes in the back of this book can also help to stimulate your thoughts.

Five Job Skills Worksheets follow. Use the same five experiences here that you have used on the Work Experience Worksheets and the Accomplishments Worksheets. Concentrate here on "what it takes to do this job," even if the "job" is part-time or unpaid. You have skills that you have learned or applied in every position you have held. This is the place where you can express them.

JOB SKILLS WORKSHEET

Job title (or position held): _____

What skills did you use in this position? What skills have you learned that you can take with you to a new position?

1.

2.

3.

Add "action words." If possible, rewrite each skill you listed above so that it begins with an action word.

1.

2.

3.

Add "facts and figures." If you haven't included specifics, now is the time to add them if you can. Rewrite each skill so that it is as "fact filled" as possible.

1.

2.

3.

Add "keywords." Look over your keywords list, assess whether any of them can be included under the heading of "job skills," and then included them below in your final rewriting.

1.

2.

3.

Congratulations again! Now you're ready to write a summary of who you are and what you have to offer to a new employer.

JOB SKILLS WORKSHEET

Job title (or position held): _____

What skills did you use in this position? What skills have you learned that you can take with you to a new position?

1.

2.

3.

Add "action words." If possible, rewrite each skill you listed above so that it begins with an action word.

1.

2.

3.

Add "facts and figures." If you haven't included specifics, now is the time to add them if you can. Rewrite each skill so that it is as "fact filled" as possible.

1.

2.

3.

Add "keywords." Look over your keywords list, assess whether any of them can be included under the heading of "job skills," and then included them below in your final rewriting.

1.

2.

3.

Congratulations again! Now you're ready to write a summary of who you are and what you have to offer to a new employer.

■ ■ ■ ■ ■ ■ ■ ■ ■ ■ ■ ■ ■ ■ ■ ■ ■ ■

JOB SKILLS WORKSHEET

Job title (or position held): _____

What skills did you use in this position? What skills have you learned that you can take with you to a new position?

1.

2.

3.

Add "action words." If possible, rewrite each skill you listed above so that it begins with an action word.

1.

2.

3.

Add "facts and figures." If you haven't included specifics, now is the time to add them if you can. Rewrite each skill so that it is as "fact filled" as possible.

1.

2.

3.

Add "keywords." Look over your keywords list, assess whether any of them can be included under the heading of "job skills," and then included them below in your final rewriting.

1.

2.

3.

Congratulations again! Now you're ready to write a summary of who you are and what you have to offer to a new employer.

JOB SKILLS WORKSHEET

Job title (or position held): _____

What skills did you use in this position? What skills have you learned that you can take with you to a new position?

1.

2.

3.

Add "action words." If possible, rewrite each skill you listed above so that it begins with an action word.

1.

2.

3.

Add "facts and figures." If you haven't included specifics, now is the time to add them if you can. Rewrite each skill so that it is as "fact filled" as possible.

1.

2.

3.

Add "keywords." Look over your keywords list, assess whether any of them can be included under the heading of "job skills," and then included them below in your final rewriting.

1.

2.

3.

Congratulations again! Now you're ready to write a summary of who you are and what you have to offer to a new employer.

■ ■ ■ ■ ■ ■ ■ ■ ■ ■ ■ ■ ■ ■ ■ ■ ■ ■ ■

JOB SKILLS WORKSHEET

Job title (or position held): _____

What skills did you use in this position? What skills have you learned that you can take with you to a new position?

1.

2.

3.

Add "action words." If possible, rewrite each skill you listed above so that it begins with an action word.

1.

2.

3.

Add "facts and figures." If you haven't included specifics, now is the time to add them if you can. Rewrite each skill so that it is as "fact filled" as possible.

1.

2.

3.

Add "keywords." Look over your keywords list, assess whether any of them can be included under the heading of "job skills," and then included them below in your final rewriting.

1.

2.

3.

Congratulations again! Now you're ready to write a summary of who you are and what you have to offer to a new employer.

CHAPTER 10

QUALIFICATIONS SUMMARY

WRITING A "CAPSULE DESCRIPTION"

Now that you know your personal skills, your personal qualifications, your experiences, your accomplishments and your "job skills," this is a good time to try to summarize them. You are going to write a "capsule description" of who you are and what you have to offer to a prospective employer. This may become the opening section of your resume or it may be included in the cover letter that accompanies your resume. (With a few modifications, it might be used in both places.)

Your goal with the "qualifications summary" is to grab an employer's attention. You want to be so interesting or so obviously qualified that an employer will want to read more about you. Your summary is a description of you "in a nutshell." Once again, you need to "think like an employer" as you write. Think about what you have to offer. Think about what will appeal to a person who is screening resumes, looking for people who might be worth interviewing.

You have already done the work for this section. Take a look back through your worksheets and see what stands out to you. It's fine to steal from what you have already written. Your Skills Worksheet is a good place to start. Maybe you will find some key words in your Personal Qualifications Worksheet that show what you have to contribute. Perhaps you have some specific "work experiences" that should be highlighted so they can't be missed. Maybe it's an accomplishment that's so impressive it's bound to interest a prospective employer or a combination of job skills that is perfect for the job you are hoping to get. Your "Keywords Worksheet" could be very useful in developing a Qualifications Summary. You might want to take a look back at it as you develop this summary.

Just as you have done in your other worksheets, you should be sure that your summary uses brief, direct phrases and includes "action words," "facts and figures," and "keywords." Several of the sample resumes at the back of this book begin with qualification summaries. You might want to glance through them to help formulate your description of yourself. Look for those that begin with a section entitled "Summary of Qualifications," "Profile," or "Summary."

QUALIFICATIONS SUMMARY WORKSHEET

Who are you? What are your skills and personal qualifications? Which of your experiences and job skills do you want an employer to know immediately? Use the spaces below to develop a brief summary of yourself.

QUALIFICATIONS SUMMARY: FIRST DRAFT

_____

_____

_____

_____

_____

_____

QUALIFICATIONS SUMMARY: SECOND DRAFT

_____

_____

_____

_____

_____

_____

QUALIFICATIONS SUMMARY: FINAL VERSION

_____

_____

_____

_____

_____

CHAPTER 11

EDUCATION

WRITING ABOUT YOUR EDUCATION AND TRAINING

Although prospective employers are usually more interested in skills, qualifications, and experience, they are also interested in education. In general, they want to know about the educational backgrounds of their potential employees. This is why nearly every resume has a section entitled "Education" (and why employers always look at this section when they review resumes).

The worksheets that follow provide a quick way for you to summarize your own education. There is a different worksheet for each level of education. If you attended college, there is no reason to complete the high school worksheet. However, if you attended graduate school, you should complete both the college and the graduate school worksheets.

If your formal education ended with high school, and you have been out of high school for more than five years, the only worksheets that you need to complete are the last three: vocational or trade school; work-related courses; and training (if any of these applies to you). If you graduated from high school within the last five years, and have not attended college, be sure to complete the high school worksheet.

Note that several of the worksheets ask you to list honors, awards, prizes; special courses or programs; and extracurricular achievements. Give some extra thought to these. Any one of them may catch the interest of an employer. Even if the award you received was for perfect attendance or for sports performance or for leadership in a student organization, it sets you apart from other job candidates and it might be something that you will want to include on your resume. Similarly, if you studied abroad or undertook any other kind of special program, note it in the appropriate place on your education worksheet.

Don't worry now about how or where this information will fit into your resume. That will be discussed when all of your worksheets—your "building blocks"—are brought together in a resume that is uniquely your own. For now, just fill out the worksheets that are right for you. It's not difficult, and it is definitely worth the effort you will put into it. Even if you don't use all of the information on your resume, you may want to use some of it in cover letters or in interviews. So turn the page and get started!

EDUCATION WORKSHEET: HIGH SCHOOL

<u>High School</u>

(NOTE: IF YOU COMPLETED MORE THAN TWO YEARS OF COLLEGE OR IF YOU ARE MORE THAN FIVE YEARS OUT OF HIGH SCHOOL, SKIP THIS SECTION.)

Name of high school _____

City and state _____

Dates attended From _____ to _____

Year of graduation _____

Grade point average (if known) _____

Rank in class (if known) _____

Honors, awards, prizes _____

Special courses or programs _____

<u>Additional high school (if you attended more than one)</u>

Name of high school _____

City and state _____

Dates attended From _____ to _____

Year of graduation _____

Grade point average (if known) _____

Rank in class (if known) _____

Honors, awards, prizes _____

Special courses or programs _____

EDUCATION WORKSHEET: COLLEGE

Name of college _____

City and state _____

Dates attended From _____ to _____

Year of graduation (or years attended) _____

Grade point average (if known) _____ Rank in class (if known) _____

Degree _____ Major or concentration _____

Additional major or concentration _____

_____

Honors, awards, prizes _____

Special courses or programs _____

Additional college (if you attended more than one)

Name of college _____

City and state _____

Dates attended From _____ to _____

Year of graduation (or years attended) _____

Grade point average (if known) _____ Rank in class (if known) _____

Degree _____ Major or concentration _____

Additional major or concentration _____

Honors, awards, prizes _____

Special courses or programs _____

EDUCATION WORKSHEET: GRADUATE SCHOOL

Name of graduate school _____

City and state _____

Dates attended From _____ to _____

Year of graduation (or years attended) _____

Grade point average (if known) _____   Rank in class (if known) _____

Degree _____ Field of study _____

Concentrations or specialties _____

Thesis or dissertation title _____

Honors, awards, prizes _____

Special courses or programs _____

Additional graduate school (if you attended more than one)

Name of graduate school _____

City and state _____

Dates attended From _____

Year of graduation (or years attended) _____

Grade point average (if known) _____   Rank in class (if known) _____

Degree _____ Field of study _____

Concentrations or specialties _____

Thesis or dissertation title _____

Honors, awards, prizes _____

Special courses or programs _____

EDUCATION WORKSHEET: VOCATIONAL OR TRADE SCHOOL

Name of school _____

City and state _____

Attended from _____ to _____ Graduation date _____

Diploma or certificate earned _____

Specialty or concentration _____

Grade point average (if known) _____ Rank in class (if known) _____

Honors, awards, prizes _____

_____

Skills learned _____

_____

Additional vocational or trade school

Name of school _____

City and state _____

Attended from _____ to _____ Graduation date _____

Diploma or certificate earned _____

Specialty or concentration _____

Grade point average (if known) _____ Rank in class (if known) _____

Honors, awards, prizes _____

_____

Skills learned _____

_____

EDUCATION WORKSHEET: WORK-RELATED COURSES

List here any courses you have taken that are job-related. These can include short courses such as workshops and seminars and longer courses, either on-the-job or in educational institutions.

Course title _____

School name _____

School address (city and state)_____

Date course was taken _____

Diploma or certificate earned_____

Honors, awards, prizes_____

_____

Skills learned _____

_____

Additional work-related courses

Course title _____

School name _____

School address (city and state)_____

Date course was taken _____

Diploma or certificate earned_____

Honors, awards, prizes_____

_____

Skills learned _____

_____

EDUCATION WORKSHEET: TRAINING

If you have received special training, either on-the-job or in an educational institution, list it here.

Special training _____

School name _____

School address (city and state) _____

Dates of training From _____ to _____

Diploma or certificate earned _____

Honors, awards, prizes _____

_____

Skills earned _____

_____

Additional training

Course title _____

School name _____

School address (city and state)_____

Date course was taken _____

Diploma or certificate earned _____

Honors, awards, prizes _____

_____

Skills learned _____

_____

EDUCATION WORKSHEET: TRAINING

If you have received special training, either on-the-job or in an educational institution, list it here.

Special training _____

School name _____

School address (city and state) _____

Dates of training From _____ to _____

Diploma or certificate earned _____

Honors, awards, prizes _____

_____

Skills earned _____

_____

Additional training

Course title_____

School name_____

School address (city andstate)_____

Date course was taken _____

Diploma or certificate earned_____

Honors, awards, prizes_____

_____

Skills learned_____

_____

CHAPTER 12

AWARDS

DOCUMENTING RECOGNITION

Awards are an excellent addition to a resume. Too many resume writers forget to include them. If you think about it, you have probably won awards in your lifetime. Some are probably work related and some may not be. Absolutely any award you have won could be listed on your resume. Ideally, the awards you include will be fairly recent (within, say, the last five years), and will communicate positively to a prospective employer (even an award for "good attendance" says something positive about you).

The Awards Worksheet lets you describe any awards you choose. The decision to include an award on your resume is yours to make. For now, put down on the worksheet any award that you are willing to discuss with a potential employer.

AWARDS WORKSHEET

Award received _____

Awarding organization _____

Date of award _____

Description of award _____

_____

Award received _____

Awarding organization _____

Date of award _____

Description of award _____

_____

Award received _____

Awarding organization _____

Date of award _____

Description of award _____

_____

Award received _____

Awarding organization _____

Date of award _____

Description of award _____

_____

CHAPTER 13

MEMBERSHIPS

ASSOCIATIONS, CLUBS, AND ORGANIZATIONS

Your memberships in professional associations, clubs, organizations, and groups can be listed on your resume. The worksheet that follows provides space for you to note these kinds of memberships. When you are trying to decide whether or not to include a membership, consider the following in making your decision:

1) Does the membership relate directly to the jobs you will be seeking?

2) Does it show your initiative outside of work—for example, a position of leadership in a volunteer role?

3) Does it communicate something about you that you don't want to state directly in another part of your resume—perhaps your race, religion, ethnic background, or physical handicap?

A WORD OF CAUTION: Although your memberships can demonstrate positive qualities about you as a candidate for a job, they also offer prospective employers the chance to discriminate against you based on the stereotypes they hold of the organizations you have joined. The opportunity for discrimination is more obvious if you list an organization that usually includes only members of specific racial or religious groups, but it is true of other types of memberships as well. A potential employer may hold negative views of any organization based on experience, hearsay, rumor, or a host of other factors. Remember to weigh these possibilities when you consider whether or not to include specific memberships on your resume.

Your memberships can be listed on your resume as simply the name of the organization or you can follow the name with the offices you have held, the number of years you have been a member, and even a brief description of the group itself if it is an association that is not well known. On the Memberships Worksheet you have the opportunity to list the memberships that you consider to be the most important. For each, you may note any offices you have held or special projects you have coordinated. You can also include the length of your membership if you choose.

You may decide later not to use this information on your resume (or not on every resume you create) but, for now, spend a few minutes recording your memberships. If you need more space, photocopy the worksheet or use a separate sheet of paper.

MEMBERSHIPS WORKSHEET

Name of organization _____

Number of years you have been a member _____

Offices held _____
(Add dates to each office if you think that these are important.)

_____

_____

Special projects (list your title if you held a position of leadership for the project)_____

_____

_____

_____

Name of organization _____

Number of years you have been a member _____

Offices held _____
(Add dates to each office if you think that these are important.)

_____

_____

Special projects (list your title if you held a position of leadership for the project)_____

_____

_____

MEMBERSHIPS WORKSHEET

Name of organization _____

Number of years you have been a member _____

Offices held _____
(Add dates to each office if you think that these are important.)

_____

_____

Special projects (list your title if you held a position of leadership for the project)_____

_____

_____

_____

Name of organization _____

Number of years you have been a member _____

Offices held _____
(Add dates to each office if you think that these are important.)

_____

_____

Special projects (list your title if you held a position of leadership for the project)_____

_____

_____

MEMBERSHIPS WORKSHEET

Name of organization _____

Number of years you have been a member _____

Offices held _____
(Add dates to each office if you think that these are important.)

_____

_____

Special projects (list your title if you held a position of leadership for the project)_____

_____

_____

_____

Name of organization _____

Number of years you have been a member _____

Offices held _____
(Add dates to each office if you think that these are important.)

_____

_____

Special projects (list your title if you held a position of leadership for the project)_____

_____

_____

CHAPTER 14

PUBLICATIONS

WRITING ABOUT YOUR WRITING

Have you written anything in the course of your work or education that you think a prospective employer should know about? If so, you might want to list your publications on your resume. "Publications" can range from news notes printed in your company newsletter to professional articles published in trade journals. If you have had your written words printed anywhere, they could certainly be considered "publications."

Perhaps you have been doing your "writing" on-line. It is possible that your "publications" are actually contributions to electronic journals or newsletters. These certainly "count" as publications these days. If you have contributed to such "virtual publications," and are willing to discuss your work with an employer, feel free to include this writing on the Publications Worksheet.

If you include a "Publications" section on your resume, the presentation of the information is up to you. The Publications Worksheet that follows will help you organize the information you want to present. Don't worry about the length of your entries. For now, put down all of the information that seems relevant.

Note that there is space on the worksheet to include a description of each publication, even though this is not usually included on a resume. It's here in case you feel that the title and "media" are not sufficient to describe your work.

This section may not apply to you. If it doesn't, skip it and go on to the next chapter. If it does apply, it will only take a few minutes to complete the worksheet. If you need additional worksheets, make a photocopy or use a separate sheet of paper.

PUBLICATIONS WORKSHEET

Title (or brief description) of your writing_____

_____

Title (or brief description) of publication or media in which your writing was published

_____

Date of publication (include issue number if relevant) _____

Description of this work _____

_____

Title (or brief description) of your writing_____

_____

Title (or brief description) of publication or media in which your writing was published

_____

Date of publication (include issue number if relevant) _____

Description of this work _____

_____

Title (or brief description) of your writing_____

_____

Title (or brief description) of publication or media in which your writing was published

_____

Date of publication (include issue number if relevant) _____

Description of this work _____

CHAPTER 15

PERSONAL INFORMATION

WHAT SHOULD YOU INCLUDE?

As recently as a decade ago, all resumes included a section that described what might be called "personal information." This section included things like marital status, number of children, church affiliation, health condition, etc. Today, it is against the law for employers to ask questions about race, religion, marital status and physical handicaps (unless a handicap prevents accomplishing parts of a job). In some parts of the U.S. it is also illegal to ask about personal sexual preferences as well. And, although it is not illegal, it is considered improper for a prospective employer to ask *any* questions that are not directly job-related. As a consequence, "personal information" sections of resumes have largely disappeared.

In general it is recommended that you don't include an old-fashioned "personal information" section on your resume. Including information about your marital status, children, church affiliation, etc., demonstrates to an employer that you are not aware of what information belongs on a resume today (and what doesn't belong). However, there may be things that you would like an employer to know about you that don't fit neatly into any of the categories that have been covered so far. Examples might include volunteer activities, leadership positions outside your worklife, a passionate hobby, a strong commitment to an organization or cause, and there could be many others. These can all be communicated on your resume under a heading like "personal information." In addition, if you are relocating to a new city, and you want a prospective employer to know why, you can note it in this section.

A "Personal Information" section can also be used to relate information that an employer cannot ask, but that you may see as helpful to your candidacy for a job. For example, if you are applying for a position where frequent out-of-town travel will be required, you might note on your resume: "Single, available to travel." (You can just as easily note that you are "Available to travel" without revealing your marital status.)

Similarly, if you know that your race can be an asset in the jobs you are seeking, you could include it in "personal information" by stating it directly (for example, "African American" or "Native American") or putting it indirectly through your affiliations ("Member, Puerto Rican Action Organization" or "Co-founder, local chapter of La Raza Latino Students Association").

PERSONAL INFORMATION WORKSHEET

The Personal Information Worksheet is completely optional. You don't have to fill in any information at all. If there are facts about you that you would like a prospective employer to know—and you haven't recorded them on the previous worksheets—this is the place to include them. The topics below are only suggestions. Use the space at the bottom of the form to include any information that you think is important.

Social organization memberships _____

_____

_____

Positions held in organizations _____

_____

_____

Hobbies _____

_____

_____

Awards or prizes for hobbies _____

_____

_____

Other information you might want to include on your resume _____

_____

_____

_____

_____

CHAPTER 16

REFERENCES

HOW TO
HANDLE THEM

You have probably seen resumes that include a section called "References." It is not required that you include a section of "references" in your own resume. However, you may want to put one in. "References" are usually just the names (and sometimes the addresses and phone numbers) of people who can offer comments about you to a possible employer.

Sometimes references are described as either "Work References" or "Character References" (also called "Personal References"). The first group would normally include former supervisors or co-workers who can evaluate your performance as an employee. The second group would include people who can offer an appraisal of your personal qualities. (Those in this group should not be relatives, but they can be longstanding friends.)

Most employers will want to speak with a previous employer before they offer you a job. (This is referred to as "checking references.") However, in most job fields it is not common for a prospective employer to check your references before interviewing you. Because of this, it is often more useful to have a separate printed list of your references available to hand (or mail) to an interested prospective employer than it is to take up space on your resume listing information that it is not actually needed.

EXCEPTIONS TO THE RULE

Having just stated a rule, let's look at the exceptions to it. First, if you are looking for work in a field where it is common for employers to check references before they interview candidates, you obviously need to include complete information about your references directly on your resume. You may already know this about your field or you may be able to find out simply by asking someone who is already employed in the field.

The second exception to the rule: if your references are well-known people, you may want to include them even if you are pretty sure that they won't be called before you are offered an interview. Including a person who is a "big name" reflects well on you and it intrigues a prospective employer. If including references on your resume increases your chances of getting an interview, then definitely include your references!

YOUR OPTIONS

There are three ways to handle "References" on your resume.

1) You can simply put down "References" as a heading and then say something like: "Available on request." This is frequently encountered on resumes, but it doesn't have much real value. It implies that you do have references but, frankly, your prospective employer is going to expect this anyway. There is nothing wrong with this approach, but it is unnecessary and it takes up space that might be put to better use.

2) You can use the general heading of "References" and list one to four people who could be contacted.

3) You can distinguish between "Work References" and "Personal References," including one or two people in each category.

ESSENTIAL RULES

If you choose to include the names of individuals as references on your resume, there are three important rules to follow:

1) **Be sure to talk with everyone you list before you put their names down on your resume!** You must have their permission before you include their names. They must be prepared to receive a telephone call at any time and you must be confident that they will give your prospective employer an appropriate appraisal of you. (It is a good idea to tell your references about the jobs you hope to get and you might want to "coach" them on key points that you hope they will mention if they're called.)

2) **Be sure to include all of the information that a prospective employer might want to know.** Whenever you can, include complete titles—even for your personal references—and add phone numbers. In general, references are checked by phone and not by mail, so complete mailing addresses are not necessary. If certain hours to call are best for your references, list those hours. You want to make it easy for employers to reach your references and you want to make the call convenient for your references too.

It is possible that your references may be checked by "e-mail," particularly if you are looking for work in a field in which electronic mail is a regular part of conducting business. If you are seeking a job in such a field, it's useful to include e-mail addresses for your references. Remember to check with your references to see if they are willing to give out their e-mail addresses and willing to be contacted in this way.

3) **Be sure that the information is accurate.** You must not only spell the names and addresses of your references correctly but you must be sure that the information is up to date. It is embarrassing (and potentially damaging to your candidacy) to have the phone number of a reference listed incorrectly or to have the title of a reference be out of date.

REFERENCE #1

The References Worksheet provides space for you to write down necessary information for each of your references. You probably don't need more than four references altogether, but you do need at least two. Even if you have decided not to include references on your resume, you should complete the worksheet because you will still need to have a list of references available for prospective employers.

Name _____

Title _____

Company/organization name _____

Address (use work address unless reference wants to be contacted at home)

_____

_____

Phone _____ E-mail _____

Best hours to call _____

Relationship to you _____

REFERENCE #2

Name _____

Title _____

Company/organization name _____

Address (use work address unless reference wants to be contacted at home)

_____

_____

Phone _____ E-mail _____

Best hours to call _____

Relationship to you _____

REFERENCE #3

The References Worksheet provides space for you to write down necessary information for each of your references. You probably don't need more than four references altogether, but you do need at least two. Even if you have decided not to include references on your resume, you should complete the worksheet because you will still need to have a list of references available for prospective employers.

Name _____

Title _____

Company/organization name _____

Address (use work address unless reference wants to be contacted at home)
_____

_____

Phone _____ E-mail _____

Best hours to call _____

Relationship to you _____

REFERENCE #4

Name _____

Title _____

Company/organization name _____

Address (use work address unless reference wants to be contacted at home)
_____

_____

Phone _____ E-mail _____

Best hours to call _____

Relationship to you _____

CHAPTER 17

THE JOB OBJECTIVE

IS IT FOR YOU?

Many resumes have a section headed "job objective," usually at the top, right under the name and address. However, this is not a mandatory part of a contemporary resume. If you look through the sample resumes in the back of this book, you will see relatively few job objectives. The reason that a job objective is not essential is that you will almost always mail your resume with a cover letter that identifies the position for which you're applying.

Even if you hand your resume directly to a person—and don't have a cover letter—it's likely that the person will know which position you are applying for and won't have to look at the "job objective" for a reminder.

ADVANTAGES AND DISADVANTAGES

The obvious disadvantage of including a job objective at the top of your resume is that it must reflect exactly the title of the job for which you are applying. This means that you may have to change the objective every time you want to submit a resume. One of the most common mistakes made by job seekers is to try to "get away with" submitting a resume with an inappropriate job objective. This never works!

The job objective simply has to match the job. Employers don't want prospective employees who appear to want a different job than the one for which they have applied! It is better to leave out the objective altogether than to send a resume in which the objective doesn't precisely match the job opening.

The advantage of including a job objective is that you just might catch an employer's attention if your objective is an exact match with the title of the job you are seeking. In this era of electronically scanned resumes, the objective also provides an opportunity to include "keywords" in your resume. If you can make your job objective match exactly the title of a specific job for which you are applying, and perhaps include some keywords as well, you could look like a strong contender right at the top of your resume.

If you plan to look for only one kind of position, it might make sense to include a job objective in your resume. If you are planning to print out of your word processor a new resume every time you apply for a job, it might also be worthwhile to include a job objective, since you can "customize" your resume every time you print it. However, if you are going to be applying for a variety of positions, and you are hoping to use one resume for several jobs, it makes more sense to include a "Qualifications Summary" in place of a job objective.

DEVELOPING YOUR JOB OBJECTIVE

Use the space provided on the Job Objective Worksheet to put your job objective into words. Try beginning with a phrase like this: "Seeking a position as..." or "Looking for a job in..." Be as specific as possible. If you find that you sound vague or general, abandon your efforts and be content with your "Qualifications Summary." For example, "Seeking a position as administrative assistant." is a good place to start if you know the title of the job you will be looking for. If you're not quite sure of the title, but you know the job field, you might consider an objective like: "Looking for an entry-level job in advertising."

To add a little more impact, you can add information about yourself. Try borrowing a phrase or two from your "Qualifications Summary." For example: "Experienced administrative assistant, with three years of progressively responsible experience, seeks position where knowledge and skills can be applied." (Notice how this emphasizes experience, includes "facts and figures," and conveys the idea of serving an employer.) Our inexperienced job seeker might try something like: "Creative, hard-working young person seeks entry-level position in advertising."

AVOIDING COMMON MISTAKES

Remember that your job objective must make you look like a person who can make a useful contribution. The most devastating (and, unfortunately, the most common) mistake you can make in a job objective is to focus on your own needs instead of focussing on the needs of your employer-to-be. Typical examples of this kind of mistake include phrases like: "Seeking rewarding position..."; "Looking for a position that offers rapid advancement..."; "Seeking a job that allows relocation to Sunbelt region..."; "Looking for a position that promises financial compensation commensurate with my experience...," etc.

The emphasis in the statements above is on the employee, and not on the employer. Although there is not one correct way to write a job objective, there is one way to go terribly wrong: talking about what you want instead of what you have to offer. If you can't write a job objective that makes you look immediately like a worker with something to offer, stick with the "Qualifications Summary" and forget the "Job Objective."

JOB OBJECTIVE WORKSHEET

You probably won't get your job objective worded perfectly on your first try, so there is space below to try three times. An additional worksheet is available too, either to develop additional job objectives or to rewrite your first one until it sounds just right. Several of the sample resumes at the end of this book include job objectives. You might want to look through these before you try to write your own.

JOB OBJECTIVE (First draft)

_____

_____

_____

_____

JOB OBJECTIVE (Second draft)

_____

_____

_____

_____

JOB OBJECTIVE (Final version)

_____

_____

_____

_____

Questions to ask in evaluating your "job objective."
—Will my objective immediately position me as a qualified candidate for the positions I am seeking?
—Does it emphasize the contribution I can make to a company or organization?
—Will it interest an employer in reading the rest of my resume?

■ JOB OBJECTIVE WORKSHEET

You probably won't get your job objective worded perfectly on your first try, so there is space below to try three times. An additional worksheet is available too, either to develop additional job objectives or to rewrite your first one until it sounds just right. Several of the sample resumes at the end of this book include job objectives. You might want to look through these before you try to write your own.

JOB OBJECTIVE (First draft)

_____

_____

_____

_____

JOB OBJECTIVE (Second draft)

_____

_____

_____

_____

JOB OBJECTIVE (Final version)

_____

_____

_____

_____

Questions to ask in evaluating your "job objective."
—Will my objective immediately position me as a qualified candidate for the positions I am seeking?
—Does it emphasize the contribution I can make to a company or organization?
—Will it interest an employer in reading the rest of my resume?

CHAPTER 18

ASSEMBLING YOUR RESUME

BRINGING THE PIECES TOGETHER

Here is the chapter you have been waiting for! Your "building blocks" are complete and it's time to assemble your resume. Since you have all of the pieces, you can assemble your resume in exactly the way you choose. This approach allows you to create one resume to use throughout your job search or it permits you to design a "customized" version every time you need a resume!

You don't have to use everything you have written. There may be items on your worksheets that you want to leave off your resume altogether. There may be entire worksheets that you don't want to include. These are your decisions.

There are very few strict rules to follow in creating a resume. There is not one "right way" to do it. Everything that follows is advice, but it is not rigid advice. Nobody knows your strengths and capabilities better than you do. Remember your goal when you are designing your resume: its purpose is to get you an interview. You want to appear to be so ideally suited for a job that you simply must be interviewed. Whether you send your resume by mail, by fax, or by e-mail, your goal is the same. With that thought in mind, let's start building your resume.

STARTING OFF

Start off your resume with your name, address, and phone number at the top of the page. Remember that electronic scanners prefer to have all of this information stacked up, one line at a time, in the upper left-hand corner. Because you don't know whether or not your resume will be electronically scanned, it is better to play it safe and follow the preferred format: one line each for name, street address, city/state/zip code, and phone number. (If you include more than one phone number, each should get its own line.)

Since prospective employers are likely to want to call you during regular business hours, try to provide a phone number where you can be reached during the day. If you can't be reached during the work day, list your home phone and, if possible, list a number where a message can be left for you on weekdays. (You may want to consider purchasing or borrowing an answering machine, contracting with an answering service for the duration of your job search, or securing an electronic "mail box" from your local phone company.) If you simply cannot be contacted during normal working hours, note next to your phone number the hours that are best to reach you.

If you have a fax number that prospective employers can use to contact you, include this under your phone number. This is also the place to list your electronic mail address if you are willing to be contacted by e-mail.

NOTE: It is not necessary to label your resume with the word "Resume" up at the top. The people who receive your resume will almost certainly know what it is.

JOB OBJECTIVE VS. QUALIFICATIONS SUMMARY

As we discussed in the section on writing a job objective, it is not necessary to have an objective on your resume. Only when your job objective matches the position you are applying for does the job objective really "work." The problem with having an objective that doesn't correspond directly with your target job is that it looks like you prepared your resume with a different job in mind. This raises concerns in the mind of your prospective employer right at the beginning of the resume.

If you are planning to look for work in only one field and you have prepared a job objective that is relevant to that field, feel free to use it at the beginning of your resume. If you are able to prepare a new resume each time you apply for a new job, you can modify your job objective so that it exactly matches the job, right down to the job title. Otherwise, you might consider a "Qualifications Summary" instead (see below).

There isn't much point in vague job objectives like "Seeking a position that utilizes my talents" or "Want a challenging position in which I can apply my skills." Remember that employers want to know what you can do for them. Your personal goals aren't all that important here. We are talking about the prime position on your resume—the first impression that an employer will have of you—and you have to make a good impression. Avoid saying what you hope to get from a job and focus instead on what you have to contribute!

After you completed your skills, personal qualifications, "work experience," accomplishments, and job skills worksheets, you compiled a summary of your qualifications—the qualities that make you an asset to an employer. You might begin your resume with this "Qualifications Summary." Look back at it now and evaluate it as a way to start off your resume.

Here is the key question to ask yourself as you assess your Qualifications Summary: Does it communicate to a potential employer your skills, personal qualifications, or experience in a way that makes you look like a person who could make a contribution to an employer? If the answer is "yes," consider starting your resume with this statement. You could call it "Qualifications" or "Summary" or "Profile" or you could make up your own category. You might also include it with no heading at all. Because it is at the top of your resume, it will be seen (and read) by everyone. Obviously, this is the perfect place to "introduce" yourself to a possible employer.

EMPHASIZING YOUR ASSETS

After you have stated your job objective or provided a summary of your qualifications, it's time to put forth your strongest qualifications for the jobs you want. These will be different for each resume writer. Fortunately, all you have to do is choose from what you have already written. Look back over your skills worksheets, your personal qualifications worksheets, your accomplishments worksheets, your experience worksheets, and your education worksheets. Which one set is likely to be most important to your prospective employers?

Traditionally, resume writers have concentrated on their experiences, but this has not always served them well. If your experience isn't very extensive, or isn't very impressive, why give it such a prominent position in your resume? Your skills, qualifications, or accomplishments might give your resume a much better start. It is often better to begin with one of these anyway, since employers will always continue to read down your resume until they find your experience and your education. Knowing that, you can save these two categories until the end of your resume if they are not your greatest assets.

Here are some guidelines to follow. These are only suggestions, and

you should feel free to ignore them. Your goal is to present your qualifications in the order you think is right for you. You are the one who decides how you are going to present yourself on paper to possible employers. If you are still uncertain after studying the guidelines below, ask some colleagues or friends which of your "building blocks" looks like the most solid way to begin the main portion of your resume.

GUIDELINES FOR EMPHASIZING YOUR ASSETS

1. Experience: If you are looking for a job that is closely related to previous jobs you have held, consider putting your experience first.

2. Accomplishments: If you have some impressive accomplishments to your credit (whether they are work-related or not), you might want to list these first, just to get the reader's attention. If they arouse curiosity about you, they will keep the reader reading.

3. Education: If you have recently graduated from college or have recently acquired a degree, diploma, or certificate that is directly related to the work you are seeking, think about stating that right at the beginning. This is especially true if you don't feel that you have impressive skills, qualifications, accomplishments, or experience.

If you are presently enrolled in an educational program that is directly related to the job you are hoping to obtain, you can treat this just as if you already had a certificate or degree. Just note that you are "presently enrolled" and then list the type of program, the subjects of courses, honors or awards, and other information that is relevant to an employer. If you are attending school while you are working (even if you are taking courses without formal enrollment in a program), include that fact on your resume.

If you do put your education first, try to include a mention of particularly important classes, your grade point average (if it is higher than a "B"), your class rank (if it is in the top 20% or so), and other facts that highlight your educational achievements. See the sample resumes for examples of how others have handled this.

4. Skills: If you have a skills list that is especially appealing to a prospective employer (and you probably do), it is always a good way to begin. You want your skills list to interest an employer enough to keep reading your resume. Most lists draw a reaction something like this: "These skills look like ones we could use." If yours is likely to get a similar response, put your skills list first. Remember to look back at both your "personal skills" and your "job skills." Both of these can be used in a section headed "Skills" on your resume.

5. Personal qualifications: Even if you don't think that you have a great deal to offer, you do have your personal qualifications. These are defi-nitely an asset; they are uniquely yours; and they are a fine place to start a resume. Maybe you are looking for your first job; maybe you are returning to work after a long absence; or maybe you are changing careers to an area in which you have no previous experience. Your personal qualifications may be the perfect place to begin.

As you will see on the sample resumes, you don't have to call your personal assets "personal qualifications." You can title this section "Profile," or "Strengths," or "Skills," or "Summary"—or you can make up any other heading you like. The point is to draw attention to your strengths as a candidate, whatever they may be.

ADDITIONAL ASSETS

Now that you have selected the section that you think presents you most favorably to a possible employer, you can let the other sections fall into place below that one. Look over your worksheets for experience, skills, qualifications, accomplishments, and education. Decide whether there are any you want to leave out altogether and then put the rest into the order that best presents your strengths.

Remember that employers are likely to keep reading until they find your experience and your education, so put those after your skills, qualifications, and accomplishments, unless they are more important than the other possible sections.

AWARDS, MEMBERSHIPS, PUBLICATIONS

After you have included all of the information listed under "Additional Assets" above, it's time to take a look at the rest of your worksheets and put them into the order of their importance. If you have completed these worksheets, take a look at them now and decide how you would like to order them in your resume. You don't have to include them at all, but try to work them into this first draft. You can see how you like them later and delete them then if they don't add enough to your resume.

PERSONAL INFORMATION

As we discussed when you completed the Personal Information Worksheet, including any personal information on your resume is entirely optional. You should not feel obligated to include this information. However, if you feel that it is a boost to your candidacy for a position, this is the place to include it. Before you do, though, read through the short chapter that precedes the worksheet to be clear on all of the guidelines for listing "personal information."

REFERENCES

Look back at the references worksheet you prepared, and look at the introduction to the worksheet too. If you want to include your references—the names, titles, addresses, phone numbers, and e-mail addresses of people who can speak to potential employers about you—they should go here at the end of your resume.

If you are not planning to put names onto your resume, you can either leave the "references" section out altogether or you can include a line that says "References available on request." If you do add such a line, you will want to be sure that you have a printed list of references available in case an employer requests one. Remember that a "References" section is not mandatory. If you don't want to include one, or if it is just taking up space on your resume, leave it out.

CONFIDENTIALITY

You might want your resume to be kept "confidential" for a variety of reasons. The most obvious is that you don't want your present employer to know that you are looking for another job. If you want your resume to be considered a confidential document, you should state that on the resume itself.

You can put a note at the top of the first page of your resume that states "CONFIDENTIAL RESUME" or simply "CONFIDENTIAL."

It is also common to include a note at the end of your resume. It can actually have a heading of its own if you choose, followed by a statement like "This resume is submitted in confidence. Please respect its confidentiality." A clear note at the bottom of your resume can be sufficient. It might state: "Please do not contact present employer without notifying candidate." A straightforward declaration is also appropriate: "Please respect the confidentiality of this resume." If confidentiality is important to you, select any of these options to deal with your concern.

SUMMARY

That wasn't so difficult, was it? Assembling your resume is really just a matter of selecting the information that you want to have an employer know about you and presenting it in the order you think is strongest. You have all the "pieces" of your resume on your worksheets. Your task now is to piece them together into a resume. Remember that you can rearrange the sections, or the material in any of the sections, to meet the requirements of each job you apply for. That's the beauty of this approach.

If you want to see some of the many ways in which resumes can be presented, take a look at the samples at the end of this book. These are only suggestions. The possibilities are nearly endless. Ultimately, you can choose exactly how you want to assemble your resume, because no one is more of an expert on the subject of you than you are.

CHAPTER 19

PRINTING YOUR RESUME

ON PAPER AND ON-LINE

After all of the time that you have put into wording your resume, it still has to look good. You want it to make a good impression. And to make a good impression, it has to be inviting to read. Even if you have assembled a terrific resume, it still has to look terrific to get noticed. It's not enough that every word is well chosen and spelled correctly. The appearance of your resume is important. Because your resume will usually be compared with many others, it needs to be competitive. It has to help you stand out from the competition.

Your resume doesn't have to command attention with dramatic graphic design or eye-catching typefaces, but it does have to be easy to read, well-organized, and "reader friendly." It is worth putting some time into the appearance of your resume. Spend a few minutes right now and read through the suggestions below.

USE A WORD PROCESSOR FOR "INPUT"

The first step in preparing a polished version of your resume, whether it will be printed or electronically transmitted, is to have it typed on a word processor. You can do this directly from the worksheets you have prepared in earlier sections of this book or you can write out a version by hand that puts everything in exactly the order you want. If you have access to a computer with word-processing software, and you are a decent typist, you can enter all of your information by yourself. If you don't have access to a computer, or aren't a very good typist, you might know someone who can help you out. If you don't have a friend—or a friend of a friend—who can enter your resume into a word processor, you can turn to a typing, word processing, or secretarial service in your community. You can find this kind of help listed in your local telephone directory.

It might take a couple of tries to get everything to look just right and to fit properly. You will also need to do some proofreading to check for spelling mistakes. Most word processing systems have built-in "spell checkers" that can check the spelling once the resume has been typed, but you will still need to check the overall accuracy. If you are not a good speller or proofreader, get some help from someone who is. If you have used a professional service, it should be able to provide help with this checking.

USE A LASER PRINTER FOR "OUTPUT"

All of the entering of information into the word processor is known as "inputting." You are putting information in. The next stage is the "outputting." In most cases this means printing, but you may also be preparing a resume for electronic transmission. Whether you do the typing yourself or have someone do it for you, and whether you are planning to print your resume or send it by electronic mail, you will probably want to do your proofreading on the "output"—a printed piece of paper (also known in computer-speak as "hard copy"). It is easier to "proof" your resume on paper, because you will be able to see it as an employer will be likely to see it. You will be able to check everything about both appearance and wording.

Some computer printers that are hooked up to word processors are able to produce different typefaces, and in different sizes as well. By using one of these "laser" printers, you or your typist can manipulate the appearance of the type on the page to get just the "look" you want. You will find a variety of resumes in the sample pages that follow. You might want to find one or more samples that appeal to you so that you can use them as models when you prepare your own.

If you do not have access to a laser printer that is capable of giving you the kind of printed version you want, you still have options available. If you can get a diskette from the word processor, you should be able to take it to a business in your community that has the kind of printer you need to produce the resume you want. You might take samples from this book to show to the person who will be formatting the "output" to get the results you are looking for. If you don't know where to turn for a high-quality printout of your resume, check your local telephone directory under headings like "typesetting," "desktop publishing," or "printing." Often these same businesses can help you get your resume printed or copied as well (see below).

PRINTING OR PHOTOCOPYING?

When you have one copy of your completed resume, just the way you want it, you can have additional copies made. You can either have them printed or photocopied. Photocopying is cheaper and faster and can often produce excellent copies. Professional printing will always produce outstanding copies (if your original is outstanding) but it may not be worth the extra expense to you.

Generally, if you are planning to have fewer than 100 copies made, turn to a photocopying service that uses high-speed, high-quality copy machines. These copies cost only a few cents apiece and should look nearly as good as your original. Copy services offer a choice of papers, sometimes with matching envelopes (see the next section for more information on paper selection), and they can often do the copying while you wait. You can also ask to see what a copy will look like on different papers and—for a very small charge—the copy service will run these for you so that you can decide which you like best. If you are not sure where you can find a copy service, check your local telephone directory under such headings as "photocopying" or "copy and duplicating services."

If you are planning to have more than 100 copies made, you can still use a photocopying service, but you might also investigate "offset printing" too. There are at least three reasons to consider using a printing service instead of a copying service:

1) You have designed a resume that will be difficult to reproduce well on a photocopier, either because of the typefaces you have selected or because of the surface texture of the paper you want to use (photocopying works better on smooth papers than on textured papers);

2) You work in a field that values appearances highly (graphic arts, computer graphics, fine arts, or any design-related field for example);

3) You are seeking a high-level position (middle manager or above), in which other applicants are quite likely to have well-designed and well-printed resumes.

Fortunately, printers frequently offer a range of printing services and can usually advise you on the type of

printing that will best meet your needs. Take your "original" with you to a commercial printer, tell the printer how many copies you are planning to have printed and the kind of paper you want to use, and ask for advice. In one shop these days you may find both copying and printing services. If you don't know of a printing service in your local community, check your telephone directory under such headings as "printers" or "copying and duplicating services." Some printing and photocopy shops that do a lot of resume printing often advertise or list themselves under the heading of "resume preparation services."

SELECTING PAPER

The paper you select for the printing of your resume is not vital to the success of the resume. Resumes that are cleanly printed on plain white paper, and meet all of the criteria outlined on the "Resume Checklist" that follows this chapter, can be just as well received by potential employers as those that are printed on colored and textured paper and arrive in matching envelopes, with cover letters computer-printed on matching paper. However, it is true that employers receive many resumes, especially for advertised positions (where it is common to receive dozens or even hundreds of responses). Although they try to select candidates to interview based on what is on the paper (and not the paper itself) it is hard not to be influenced by appearances. This is especially true in businesses where appearances are an important part of the work, such as design and art-related enterprises, architecture, interior decorating, and similar ventures.

Generally speaking, it costs very little more money to have your resume copied or printed onto a colored paper than onto white paper. Some copy services and printers stock envelopes to match selected papers, and all will be happy to sell you extra sheets of the paper you select for your resume so that you can use matching paper for your cover letters. Ask to see available papers and ask directly about the comparative costs before you make your selection.

CHOOSING A PAPER COLOR

As far as color, keep it conservative unless you know that you will be looking for work in a job field that values creativity. In most fields it is fine to stand out a little in a pile of resumes, but it is not OK to stand out a lot. Off-white paper colors and so-called "neutrals" are safe choices if you want to move away from white. These may have names like "cream," "tan," "buff," "ivory," etc. Very pale shades of blue are also fine. If you are in doubt about a color, stay with a light one.

There are several other reasons these days to stay with a light-colored paper that has very little texture to it (in other words, a "smooth-finish" paper). First, it is likely that your resume will be photocopied after it is received by a prospective employer. Light col-

ors tend to come out of copy machines as white, leaving your resume looking pretty much like the "original" that you sent. Darker colors (blue, gray, green, etc.) tend to come out of the copier as a muddy gray color, with the type appearing to fade into the paper (not a good way to make a positive impression with the people who receive the photocopied version of your resume).

The second reason to keep the paper color light (and the ink dark) is the "fax" machine. Like photocopiers, fax machines "read" the contrasts between light and dark colors. They transmit better copies when the contrast of colors on the original is most distinct. There is an increasing chance that you or an employer will fax your resume and you will want the fax to transmit as cleanly as possible.

A third reason to keep the paper light and smooth is the use of "scanners." As you learned in the early chapters of this book, these machines optically "scan" your resume and enter it into a computerized database. This practice is growing in corporations both large and small. Like copiers and fax machines, scanners produce their best results when there is the greatest contrast between paper and ink.

The moral here is: keep the paper light and the ink dark when you're printing your resume.

For your cover letters, it is a nice touch—but certainly not necessary—to use the same paper that you use for your resume. You can purchase extra sheets of paper inexpensively when you have your resume printed and you can type your cover letters directly onto these sheets (or put the sheets into the printer for your word processor). Again, this is not essential. It is just another way to make you look attractive as a job candidate and you should take advantage of the opportunity if you can.

SELECTING ENVELOPES

It is not essential that you have matching envelopes (since your envelope is likely to be tossed out as soon as it is opened) so this is one place where you can save some money. Similarly, you don't need to have envelopes printed with your name and address on them. This is expensive and not usually necessary (unless you are looking for a very high level job). However, it is important that your envelopes be typed and not handwritten. Handwritten envelopes, of any size, just don't make a good impression. Although it is true that most people who are doing the actual hiring for a job don't see the envelopes that contain resumes (since someone else usually opens the envelopes), why take a chance?

One investment that is definitely worth considering (and it is a small additional expense) is the purchase of envelopes that are larger than standard business envelopes. The standard business envelope requires you to fold your resume and cover letter twice to fit it into the envelope. The much larger 9"

x 12" envelope allows you to insert both cover letter and resume without a fold at all. This is especially important today, when job seekers have to consider the possibility that their resumes will be faxed or scanned.

Neither fax machines or scanners can operate at their best with pages that have been folded. Even photocopiers often have trouble with folds. If the fold line falls on a line of type, it is quite likely that the words on that line will not transmit clearly. It's not worth gambling. If you can, take the time to find envelopes that will enclose your resume and cover letter without folding. Large envelopes are available in most office supply stores. Look for those that are not the standard brown color if you want to make your resume stand out in the mail.

The larger- size envelope may help your envelope be opened before others. But it is the fold lines that are the most important reason to think about using a large envelope. The extra effort you make to ensure that your resume (and cover letter) arrive in great condition can pay off for you in ways that you can't foresee. It's another way to get a jump on the competition.

CUSTOMIZING YOUR RESUME

Just as cover letters need to be individualized every time you send out your resume, it can be argued that your resume is most effective if it is customized to the job every time you mail it. Because every job has slightly different requirements, you might emphasize slightly different experiences or qualifications each time you apply for a position. If you have easy access to a word processor and are pretty good at using it—or you have a friend or colleague who can do the work for you at a reasonable cost—you might consider reshaping your resume every time you apply for a job. And if you are going to send your resume electronically, you will definitely want to customize it, since it will probably be sent directly from the same computer that is used to prepare it.

Customizing your resume is not as difficult (or as wacky) as it might sound. When you know the requirements for a particular position you simply evaluate your resume, and the worksheets you used to prepare it, to see if you have presented yourself as a well-qualified candidate. Sometimes you will want to reorder your qualifications. Other times you may choose to expand the description of a particular experience that is especially relevant. You may decide to change your objective or your summary of qualifications every time you apply for a job. You may want to add or subtract "keywords" as well. The word processor allows you to move text around quickly and the worksheets you completed earlier in this book give you the additional material you might want to use.

To print your customized resume, you can "output" directly from the word processor's printer onto nearly any paper you choose or you can go

through any of the steps outlined above to produce a printed version. Obviously this approach makes the most sense when the word processor's printer is able to produce a product you feel is ready to send. With this capability you can easily produce individualized resumes as well as individualized cover letters—and print both on the same paper as well. You can also produce a resume that is ready for electronic transmission.

If you are planning to look for work in more than one career field, you will probably need more than one version of your resume. It is common for job seekers to have a different version for each type of job they are seeking. You don't have to "customize" your resume for every individual job, as we discussed above, but you will want to have different resumes for different types of positions. For example, if you are planning to apply for jobs in sales and in marketing, you may want to consider having two resumes—one that emphasizes your qualifications and experiences in sales and one that highlights your qualifications and experiences in marketing. You can have these photocopied or printed and you can even have them put onto the same type of paper if you want to. Just remember which resume is which and use them accordingly.

"ELECTRONIC RESUMES"

Each of the first three chapters of this book discussed, among other topics, the impact of computerized systems on resume design today. One new technology that is having an immediate impact on resumes is "electronic mail." So-called "e-mail" allows resumes to be sent directly from one computer to another. This means that job seekers can prepare their resumes with the help of their computers' word processing software, transfer them into e-mail systems, and send them off electronically to almost any computer in the world.

If the receiving computer is hooked into a resume tracking or management system, the received resumes can be electronically checked to see if they were transmitted without errors. They are then "filed" in a computer which can "search" the entire database of resumes for "keywords" that match key hiring characteristics for available jobs. When resumes are selected through a computerized search, they can be forwarded directly to the computer of the person who will be selecting, interviewing, and hiring candidates. All of this could happen within minutes—and it might never use a single piece of paper! This is what has been called a "resume revolution."

If the resume revolution hasn't affected you yet, it might be just a matter of time before you feel its effects. The electronic transmission of resumes is not restricted only to high-tech occupations, although it is already common there. Millions of people now have access to e-mail and several thousand a day are "logging on" for the first time. "What's your e-mail address?" is a question that is heard frequently today and it is likely to be heard even more frequently in the future. It is quite possible that you might be asked to e-mail your resume the next time that you apply for a job. And it is just as possible for people applying for jobs in small firms as for people applying to large companies.

HOW TO "E-MAIL" YOUR RESUME

So what do you do if you are asked by an employer or recruiter to "e-mail" your resume? If you don't have access to e-mail from your computer (or if you don't have a computer), you ask if you can send your resume by mail, by fax, or by overnight express instead. You won't be the only job candidate who doesn't have e-mail and your candidacy shouldn't be hurt by your lack of electronic capability.

If you do have a computer and access to e-mail, you should be able to send your resume electronically. You might need a little help the first time you try, but a trustworthy (and computer-literate) co-worker or friend can probably lend a hand. Basically, you will be transferring your resume as a document from your word processor, where it is stored, to your e-mail, which can send it to another computer. You might be asked to send it without the formatting codes that your word processor automatically puts into documents (the request might be worded like this: "Will you strip out the formatting codes?" or this: "Will you send that to me in ASCII?"). This request is made so that the receiving computer can deal with the "text" of the resume without having to deal with the codes that control such items as paragraph breaks, typefaces, underlined words, etc. (this format is also known as "raw text").

You can probably remove the formatting codes from your resume by yourself if you are asked to do so. It is common for word processing software to offer the option of "translating a file into ASCII"—which is computer-speak for removing the codes. If you are not sure whether your word processor offers such an option, check the documentation manuals, talk with a colleague who uses the same word processor, call the "help line" of the software manufacturer, or ask at the computer store where the computer or software was purchased.

As e-mail systems have become more sophisticated, their text-processing capabilities have grown. It is possible that your system can remove the codes from a document before it is "mailed." Again, check the manuals that explain your e-mail system (look for a heading like "document handling" or "document transfer"), talk with a colleague, call the "help line," or ask at a computer store.

When the formatting codes are removed from your resume, it becomes simply a collection of words. The words stay in order but all of the

"design" of your resume is lost. (Computerized resume search systems are not at all interested in design features; they are concerned only with words.) Your resume becomes simply a "document." This fact alone emphasizes the importance of the words you choose for your resume. Obviously they need to be spelled correctly. And "keywords" for a specific job or occupational field are vital, because the text of your resume will be searched on-line by keywords.

You probably won't be able to avoid printing copies of your resume—and you probably don't want to have a resume that is never printed. However, the days of using only a printed resume that is sent through the mail or dropped off at a place of business are long gone. Today intelligent job seekers understand the need to customize their resumes. It may well be that you will develop a slightly different resume every time you apply for a job! Some of your resumes will be conventionally mailed, while others will be faxed, sent by overnight express, or "e-mailed."

COPING WITH CHANGING TIMES

As a job seeker, you have to change with the times, and the times are a'changing. If you are having trouble adjusting to the changes, remember that your resume is still a vital part of your job search today. In fact, it is hard to imagine conducting a job search today without a resume. And the words you choose to put on the resume are more important than ever. They are no longer read only by people, but now computers are "reading" them as well. The methods for sending, receiving, and storing them are growing in variety (and in complexity too). But resumes are alive and well. And the new ways to design, modify, and send them present a wealth of new opportunities.

Don't worry. With a little learning, you will be able to take advantage of the new technologies. In only a short time, you will be customizing your resume for a specific job and e-mailing it off to a prospective employer as if there had never been another way. Don't be intimidated by the technology. It's just a new tool for the educated job seeker (like yourself).

A note about "faxes": Remember that if you fax your resume, it is a good idea to send an "original" by mail or overnight express. Because it is increasingly likely that your resume will be photocopied or electronically scanned after it is received, you want your prospective employer to receive a very "clean" copy. Faxed documents, including resumes, are often received in poor condition and their condition is further degraded by photocopying or scanning. Photocopies of faxes are frequently difficult for humans to read and scanners almost always have trouble "reading" faxes accurately. Whether your resume is headed for a desk or into a computer, you want it to be easily deciphered. Whenever you are asked to send a fax (or decide to send one because it will arrive quickly), follow up with a paper "original."

CHAPTER 20

RESUME TIPS

SUGGESTIONS FOR EVERY RESUME

Here are a few suggestions that can improve your resume. The "do" and "don't" format is easy to understand. Follow these simple tips and you will craft a resume that really works for you!

DO!

1. "Grab" your readers. Start your resume off with a bang! At the top of your resume, right under your name, address, and phone number, include some key points about yourself that will make a prospective employer want to keep reading. Make yourself look like a terrific candidate for the job you want. A summary of your accomplishments, experience, personal qualifications, or skills is an excellent way to do this.

2. Emphasize your strengths. You probably know the saying "If you've got it, flaunt it." This is certainly true on your resume. Your prospective employer should be able to quickly see what you have to offer. A summary of your best "selling points" at the top of the resume can communicate your strengths at a glance.

3. Structure your resume like a pyramid. The most important things about you should be near the top of your resume. There is no formula that you have to follow in assembling the components of your resume, but you should definitely begin with your best features. Remember that most employers will continue to read (if they like what they see) until they find your experience and education. Since you know that, you can put important facts about yourself (in order of their importance) between your name at the top and your experience or education further down your resume.

4. Be sure your resume is easy to read. If your resume is jammed with words, crammed with tiny type, or simply uninviting to a reader, no one is going to take the time to read it—even if you are a great job candidate. Remember that your resume has to be easy for computers to read too. If you have difficulty judging the appearance of your resume, ask a co-worker or friend to evaluate it for you.

5. Keep sentences short. Start as many as you can with "action words." It's OK to drop words like "a," "an," and "the."

6. Use "keywords." You need to know the "buzzwords" for the jobs you want and you need to use these words in your resume. If you can, use the

exact words and phrases that appear in job ads or job descriptions. (See the chapter on "keywords" for more details.)

7. <u>Support your objective</u>. If you have a job objective, be sure that your resume shows clearly why you are qualified for the job you are seeking. Information that doesn't relate to your job objective should be reworded so that it does relate or it should be dropped altogether.

8. <u>Make every word count</u>. Every word in your resume must be spelled correctly and every word should have a reason for being there. Remember that your resume may be electronically "scanned" and "searched." Misspelled words and extraneous words are wasted even more on computers than they are on humans.

9. <u>Keep your resume to one or two pages</u>. Most employers don't want to read more than two pages, unless you have vast (and relevant) experience. If your resume continues onto another page, tell the reader. All it takes is a simple note at the bottom of a page: "Continued on next page" or "See next page."

10. <u>Answer the question that every employer asks</u>. Your resume must address the question that is on every employer's mind: "What can this person do for me?" If your resume can answer that question, you can get an interview—and an interview can land you a job. One of the best ways to answer the question is to include summaries of your personal qualities, experience, skills, and accomplishments.

DON'T

1. <u>Don't lie</u>. You can never make a lie work in your favor. Don't stretch the truth too far either—it will break!

2. <u>Don't copy someone else's resume</u>. You are unique and your resume needs to reflect your uniqueness. You can take inspiration from other resumes, including the samples in this book, and you can borrow elements from the resumes of others, but make your resume your own.

3. <u>Don't write long sentences</u>. Remember that your resume will be read very quickly. Make sure that it can be read easily.

4. <u>Don't waste words</u>. Too many resumes are long-winded. Think like an employer when you review your resume. Drop the words and phrases that are not essential.

5. <u>Don't put more than four lines together in one "block."</u> Employers need to be able to read "at a glance." If you have more than four short lines, you are probably trying to say too much. Divide a long block of text into two points.

6. <u>Don't be vague</u>. Be as specific as possible. Include "facts and figures" wherever you can. If you are vague, be sure that you are vague on purpose (for example, you might choose to say "Service position in food service industry" instead of "Waitress in a coffee shop").

7. <u>Don't include information that is not relevant to an employer</u>. Select from your experience, accomplishments, personal qualities, and skills those that relate most closely to the job you hope to obtain. There is a good rule to follow in evaluating whether or not something is relevant: "If in doubt, leave it out."

8. <u>Don't include "personal" information</u>. There is almost never a need to include such data as your height, weight, age, marital status, number of children, etc. In fact, including information like this makes you look like you don't know what you're doing in preparing a resume. This kind of information hasn't been included in resumes for more than twenty years and most employers would be shocked and dismayed to see it.

9. <u>Don't list a reference unless you have the person's permission</u>. Of course, it's important too to know that you will get a positive recommendation!

10. <u>Don't build your resume around dates</u>. Dates should be put at the end of any description—not at the beginning—or they should be left out altogether. *When* you did anything is not as important as *what* you did. If you emphasize dates, employers will focus on dates. Don't give them the opportunity!

CHAPTER 21

THE RESUME CHECKLIST

DOES YOUR RESUME MEASURE UP?

Do you want to know how good your resume is? Do you want to be able to critique your own resume before you send it to a potential employer? Try this short "test."

If you can answer "Yes" to all of the following questions, then you have a resume that should work well for you in your job search (or in your efforts to move up in the organization you work for now). This is not the only way to evaluate your resume. You should have other people give you feedback as well: colleagues, friends, family, and (most importantly) people who are already employed in the type of job that you are seeking. Remember, though, that many people have out-of-date ideas about what a resume should look like, so some of the "advice" you receive you will have to ignore.

If you can't answer "Yes" to all of the questions here, try to see what is standing between your resume and "Yes." What can you modify on your resume so that your answer is an unqualified "Yes"? It will be well worth the time that it will take to make those changes. If you need motivation, remember that there is probably someone else looking for the same jobs that you are who can answer "Yes" to all of these questions!

1. Do you appear to be qualified for the job you are seeking?

2. Are your strongest "selling points" clearly visible?

3. Is your resume easy to read and understand?

4. Does it invite reading through good design and professional appearance?

5. Are your greatest strengths closest to the top?

6. Are dates out of the "sight line"? (If they appear at all, do they appear at the end of descriptions and on the right side; not at the beginning of descriptions, on the left side?)

7. Does each description begin with an "action word"?

8. Are your sentences short, with no wasted words?

9. Have you included "keywords" for the job you want?

10. Will your resume "scan" successfully? (Have you used simple typefaces and eliminated unnecessary ornaments?)

■ ■ ■ ■ ■ ■ ■ ■ ■ ■ ■ ■ ■ ■ ■ ■ ■ ■ ■

11. Are you prepared to discuss everything on your resume with a potential employer?

12. Have you eliminated information that could be used to discriminate against you?

13. Is everything spelled correctly?

14. Is everything grammatically correct?

15. Are your name, address, and phone number(s) easy to read and located in the upper left corner of your resume?

Congratulations! If you can answer "Yes" to the questions above, you are ready to use your resume as one of the most important parts of your job-seeking campaign.

CHAPTER 22

SPECIAL SITUATIONS

DIFFERENT STRATEGIES FOR DIFFERENT NEEDS

If you have already tried putting your resume together, you may have thought to yourself: "I think that I am in a special situation." Probably everyone who writes a resume has a "special situation" that requires its own special strategy. This chapter suggests strategies for a number of frequently-encountered "special situations." Take a look through the chapter subheadings and see if you fall into any of these groups.

Although the situations included here are certainly not comprehensive, you might discover some tips for dealing with a problem that you have encountered in writing your resume. The suggestions are only suggestions. You may invent a solution that is perfect for your situation completely on your own—but this chapter should provide you with some good ideas. Remember to study the sample resumes at the end of the book too. You might find that others have solved the same problems that you face.

1. INEXPERIENCED OR LOOKING FOR A FIRST JOB

If you lack experience, you will want to build your resume around your other "selling points." You might not even include a section entitled "Experience." What you need to do is figure out the key things about you that will be most appealing to the employers you plan to contact. You should concentrate on communicating your skills, personal qualifications, accomplishments (no matter where you achieved them), and your education (see the next section below).

2. STUDENT

If you are presently in school and looking for a full-time job (either right now or after graduation), you will not be expected to have a lot of relevant work experience. Instead, you will probably focus your resume on school-related activities. Although "Education" could be the first section on your resume, it is often advisable to start out with a description of your personal qualities (which are called "Personal Qualifications" in this book and should be included on your resume that way too). This can help to "bring you to life" for employers, most of whom are not too good at translating your student activities into job qualifications.

Your main task is to show how your courses, paid or volunteer work, and outside activities have prepared you for a full-time job. If you have leadership experience in any activity, you will want to highlight it. If you have good grades, be sure to note that on your resume. If you have managed to work, full-time or part-time, at ANY job while you have been in school, emphasize that fact (including the average number of hours per week you worked). You don't have to try to turn your part-time job as night custodian into more than it is. It is not so much the job that counts here as the fact that it shows responsibility and the ability to plan your time.

Remember that you may have to explain the importance of some of the entries on your resume. It isn't enough to note: "Night Custodian, Sports Arena." Tell why that is significant: "Worked 3-4 hours, beginning at 11:00 p.m., after every major event in arena (an average of two per week). Received citation for attendance and attention to detail."

3. REENTERING THE WORKFORCE

If you have been out of the work force for a year or more, you probably have questions about how to explain your absence. You have several options: you can leave out dates altogether on your resume and be prepared to answer questions if they come up in an interview; you can explain the absence straightforwardly on your resume ("Recovering from injuries sustained in automobile accident, July 1995 to December 1995"); or you can include dates and leave a gap of time. Employers often become

wrapped up in their attempts to put together an exact chronology of your life from your resume. One way to discourage that is to emphasize your skills, personal qualifications, and accomplishments—and provide only a list of employers and positions held, without any dates at all. This is a perfectly valid approach to resume preparation. It puts the emphasis where it should be—on you and your qualifications—and not on dates.

Although it may be tempting to explain your personal situation in detail on your resume or in your cover letter, avoid the temptation. Cover letters that begin: "I took the last six months off to raise a beautiful baby girl and now I am ready to return to work" or "I am a recovering alcoholic and have spent the last three months in intensive therapy and am now able to work" violate the cardinal rule of cover letter (and resume) writing: tell the employer what you have to offer! Stress the positive contribution you can make, not your personal life saga.

4. SEEKING PART-TIME WORK OR FLEXIBLE HOURS

The place to discuss your interest in work that is not full-time is in your cover letter, not in your resume. In fact, you should not make any distinctions on your resume. Write your resume with the help of the worksheets in this book, just as if you were seeking a full-time job. Treat the opening of your cover letter the same way, stating the kind of work you are seeking and what you have to contribute. After you have gotten the employer's attention, then bring up your interest in part-time or flexible hours.

Remember that employers are not particularly interested in your convenience. (You won't get far with a letter that begins: "Because I have a number of commitments to my family, I am interested in working only Mondays and Wednesdays between 9:00 and 3:00".) Like all job seekers, you must demonstrate how you can make a valuable contribution to the employer's organization. And you don't want to give a prospective employer a reason NOT to interview you. Bring up your special requirements in an interview and not on your resume.

5. CHANGING CAREERS

Changing careers is increasingly common, but employers still look on career changers with skepticism and tend to favor people who have worked in the employer's field over those who do not have direct work experience. However, many employers have had wonderful experiences with career changers (or they at least know other employers who have had wonderful experiences) and there is more openness today to people changing careers than there has been in the past.

If you are trying to move from one career to another, you must create a resume and cover letter that demonstrate that you have the skills and personal qualifications that will allow you

to do the job you are seeking. Employers can't be expected to make the connections between your previous experience and your desired job. You have to make the connections for them.

This means that you have to understand the job requirements of the job you are hoping to get and you must understand the needs of the employer as well. Your resume should emphasize your skills and personal qualifications and the contribution you can make. If you include your previous experience, be sure to point out what you have learned that can now be transferred to a new occupation.

6. UNEMPLOYED

There shouldn't be a stigma attached to being unemployed, but it does seem that employers look more favorably on people who are presently employed than on people who are not employed (maybe they like the idea of "stealing" people away from other employers because it makes them seem more valuable.) For the unemployed job seeker, it is always hard to hide the fact that you are not presently working.

However, like people reentering the workforce after an absence (see above), you do not have to include dates on your resume if you are unemployed. Removing dates makes employers focus on what you have to offer and not on when you worked where. This is not a "trick." It is an intelligent strategy. (And it is far better than listing your most recent job in an open-ended manner on your resume: "1992 to present" for example. This approach will only embarrass you if you are called in for an interview.)

There are a lot of capable workers who are presently unemployed. You don't have to make excuses on your resume or in your cover letter. However, if you do want prospective employers to know why you are unemployed, you can note it straightforwardly: "Due to corporate consolidation, entire factory closed in March 1996," for example.

Your cover letter can also omit all mention of dates and can focus instead on your accomplishments, your experience, or on the contributions you think you can make to the employer's organization.

7. FIRED OR LAID OFF

Although you will need to be prepared to discuss your firing or layoff in a job interview, you do not need to discuss it in your resume or cover letter. If you want to state the reason for a layoff, however, there is no "rule" against it. See the suggestions above under the headings "Unemployed" and "Reentering the Workforce."

8. HANDICAPPED

The very term "handicapped" is being replaced by terms like "physically challenged," "specially challenged," or "differently abled." The

new terms seem especially appropriate when discussing job-search strategies, including writing resumes and cover letters. It is against federal (and most state) laws to discriminate against people with handicapping conditions (unless the employer can prove that certain physical abilities are an essential part of a given job). Although attitudes are changing, partly as a result of this legislation and partly from the greater presence of people with disabilities in the workforce, prejudice dies hard and prejudice against the "disabled" is still rampant.

If you are a physically challenged person, you can choose to mention that fact on your resume and in your cover letter or you can choose to ignore it. "Neglecting" to include your "disability" lets you compete directly with other candidates and reduces the chance that you will be a victim of an employer's bigotry or fear. However, you may have strong feelings about how you want to present yourself on paper. The decision is yours to make.

9. NEW CITIZEN OR NON-CITIZEN

If much of your experience and many of your accomplishments have occurred outside the United States, prospective employers may be reluctant to interview and hire you for several reasons: they may not believe that you know U.S. procedures and ways of doing business; they may worry about your language proficiency; and they may be concerned that the status of your citizenship will prove to be a problem for them.

Knowing these concerns in advance, you can address them in your resume and cover letter. At the bottom of your resume you might include a note entitled "Citizenship" or "Visa Status." In your descriptions of your experience, you might use U.S. terms wherever you can. And in a section that could be headed "Special Skills," you could announce your levels of proficiency in various languages.

Your cover letter can go into any of these areas in more detail. Before you write either your resume or your cover letter, you might want to speak with someone in your situation who has successfully found a job. You might also talk with an employer and find out exactly what concerns employers have, so that you can deal with these in your resume and cover letter.

10. EARLY RETIREE

There are many occupations from which workers traditionally retire at an age far younger than 65 and then seek new jobs. Some of the most common occupational categories include teachers, police, and people in the military. Often these workers have difficulties writing resumes because they don't know how to handle their "first" careers when they are applying for positions in their "new" career field.

Like the situations of those who are changing careers (see above),

people beginning second careers need to "build bridges" for prospective employers between their first careers and the jobs they are applying for after retirement. Generally these are people with a number of skills and well-established work habits. They can be of great value to employers. Their challenge is to demonstrate exactly how their skills and experiences can benefit their employers.

Both the resume and cover letter should make clear the kinds of contributions that the early retiree can make to employers. Thorough knowledge of the job is essential for the early retiree since it is entirely up to the applicant to persuade the employer that it is worth the time to interview this person who has already "given up" one career and now wants to begin another.

Examples of many of these special situations, and how job seekers have responded to them, exist in the sample resumes that appear at the back of this book. If you face one of these situations, you might benefit from thoroughly reading through the sample resumes.

"I'm just curious—were you on any kind of mind-expanding
medication when you wrote this resume?"

CHAPTER 23

COVER LETTERS

INTRODUCING
YOUR RESUME

There is a lot of unnecessary mystery that surrounds cover letters. Many job seekers don't seem to understand them at all. But they are actually very easy to understand—and they are very easy to write too. Basically, a cover letter "introduces" your resume. It has several simple goals: it lets an employer know WHY you are sending a resume; it tells, briefly, WHAT you have to offer; and it states HOW you hope things will proceed after the employer studies your resume. That doesn't sound very complicated, does it? Well, it isn't very complicated!

Your resume should never go into an envelope, be sent as a fax, or be transmitted electronically without a cover letter. Whether you are applying for a specific job that is currently available, inquiring about jobs that might be available now (but are unadvertised), or asking about jobs that could be available in the future, you will need a cover letter. Resumes that are received anywhere without cover letters are routinely put into wastebaskets (except at more progressive firms, where they are put into recycling bins).

The one point to hold in your mind when you write a cover letter is: "What do I have to contribute to this employer?" That is the crucial question to answer in your cover letter. The most common mistake that job seekers make in developing their cover letters is to focus on their own needs instead of on the needs of employers. They emphasize the reasons that they are applying for positions, when these reasons mean very little to employers and are not of much interest to them. What employers want to know is what you can do for them—not what they can do for you. So, to write a successful cover letter, you have to think like an employer.

PICTURE YOURSELF AS
AN EMPLOYER

When you write a cover letter, it might help you to picture yourself as an employer, sitting at a desk opening one envelope after another, each one holding a resume and a cover letter. If you're like most employers, you will start making three piles out of these resumes and cover letters: the "yes" pile (this person looks great. I have to schedule an interview); the "maybe" pile (the person I see described on paper looks kind of interesting, but not as interesting as the people in the "yes" pile); and the "NO" pile (this candidate just doesn't look qualified).

Although it sounds rather perverse, employers are usually looking for reasons to keep the "yes" pile as small as possible. They don't want to interview lots of people if they can find their next employee by interviewing only a few people. So they find themselves looking for reasons to put candidates into the "maybe" or "no" piles. You don't want your cover letter to give them an excuse to keep you out of the "yes" pile.

The biggest challenge that you face as a job seeker is to get your cover letter and resume into an employer's "yes" pile. A good cover letter can make the difference between landing in the "maybe" pile or ending up in the "yes" pile. Since most usually interview only those candidates in the "yes" pile, your cover letter has a vital part to play in your job search.

EVERY RESUME GETS A COVER LETTER

Not only do you have to send out a cover letter with every resume, no matter how you send it, but you have to send a different letter out with every resume. At the very least, you will have to change the name and address of the employer and the title of the job you are applying for. When you are looking for only one kind of position, these small changes may be the only modifications you will need to make to your cover letter. However, if you are seeking different kinds of jobs, you will definitely need different types of cover letters.

Changing your cover letter every time you send it out is not quite as intimidating as it sounds. As you will see below, cover letters are not very long and they are not very difficult to write. Avoid the temptation to say the same thing in every letter you write (and definitely avoid the temptation to have one letter printed or copied to accompany every resume you send.) The extra time you spend on your cover letter can make the difference between getting called for an interview and being forgotten. If you are going to write, take the time to do it right!

HOW TO WRITE A COVER LETTER

A few crucial elements have to appear in every cover letter. Let's look at them in order. You might want to follow along with a cover letter that you have prepared or with one of the sample cover letters that appears at the end of this chapter.

Date

Here's a painless way to get started. Begin with the month, day, and year.

Employer and address

Always try to direct your cover letter and resume to a specific person, and include that person's title as well. If you don't know who the correct person is, pick up the telephone and call. It's worth the few minutes of time and the small amount of money it will cost to make the call. If you don't do it now, you will kick yourself later when you want to follow up with another letter or call. Similarly, if you are not sure of the spelling of a name or the exact title of the person, call and find out. You will hurt your chances if you don't. (Nobody likes to have a name misspelled or a title misstated.) Obviously, you need to make sure that you have the address correct as well.

Salutation

If you know the gender of the person you are addressing, a simple "Dear Ms. _____" or "Dear Mr. _____" is fine. If you don't know the gender, call and ask (you won't be the only person who has ever inquired). If you really can't find out, then write out the person's full name after the word "Dear." If you do not have a name in the address, or have only a title (like "Personnel Manager" or "Marketing Director," simply skip the salutation altogether. (The days of writing "To whom it may concern" or "Dear sir or madam" are long gone.)

First paragraph: WHY

The first paragraph has one purpose: to state exactly WHY you are writing. Are you applying for a position that was advertised? If so, where was it advertised? Are you writing without knowing about an opening? If so, why did you pick this person or organization?

The first paragraph can be very

brief, as you will see in the sample cover letters that follow.

Second paragraph: WHAT

In the second paragraph, you describe WHAT you have to offer to this particular employer. This is the most important paragraph of your cover letter. It is here that you link your qualifications to the job for which you are applying. It is also in this paragraph that you encourage the employer to take a close look at your resume (and you provide reasons for taking that look).

This paragraph will probably change from one letter to another, although you may come up with phrases that you can use in more than one cover letter. For some letters, you might want to emphasize your experience, if it is directly relevant to a position you are seeking. In another, you may want to highlight your personal qualifications, if they seem to match the requirements of the job. For still another letter, you could note your education, including specific courses that prepared you for the job you hope to secure. This is the spot where you "build a bridge" between your qualifications and the needs of the employer.

This paragraph is the "heart" of your cover letter. It shows the employer that you have thought about the job (or the organization) and believe that you can make a genuine contribution. (If you don't think that you can make a genuine contribution you probably shouldn't waste your time—and the employer's—by writing.) This is your chance to feature one or two specifics from your past that might positively impress a prospective employer. Have you taken on a project that demonstrates your initiative? Have you solved a problem in a way that saved time or money for a previous employer or organization? Have you faced challenges that are similar to those you are likely to face in this new position?

Feel free to "raid" your resume for examples and phrases. You can take any material in your resume and use it directly in your cover letter if it supports the point you want to make. You have already put a lot of effort into developing the wording of your resume and you do not have to reword it now if it works "as is." If it suits your purposes, use it. If not, rework it until it does. For example, you might want to add more detail about an accomplishment or a previous job in your cover letter than you included on your resume because the experience relates directly to the position you are applying for. One or two examples are all you need.

If you are responding to an advertisement or job description, make sure that you address the specific points that are raised there. You can even borrow some of the same phrases for your letter if it seems appropriate. For example, if an ad states that the employer is looking for someone who is "personable, able to work independently, and a quick learner," it is OK to note in your cover letter: "I am personable, able to work independently, and a quick learner." If you can back any of those statements up with specific examples, do so. If you can also refer the employer to examples on your resume, do that too.

Remember: this is the place where you establish your qualifications. You want to "hook" the reader into reading your resume to find out more about you. Don't try to condense your whole resume into a one paragraph summary. This part of the cover letter is just a "taste" of what is on the resume. Your challenge here is to make the reader want to find out more about you and to want to read your resume.

Third paragraph: HOW

This is your final paragraph. You want to let the reader know HOW to reach you to set up an interview. (Do you want to be called at work or at home? What are the best times to call?) You also want to state HOW you are going to proceed. (Are you going to call to follow up? If so, when?) Finally, you should state HOW you have responded to any specific requests the employer has made. (Were you asked to submit a sample of your previous work? A list of references?) Use this paragraph to address these requests.

Closing

Close your letter as you would any business letter. Use a businesslike closing word or phrase and follow it with your signature, your address, and your phone number(s). If you are using letterhead stationery that includes the address and phone number you want to use for contacts with prospective employers, you don't need to repeat the information in your closing.

You will find different closing words on the sample cover letters that follow. Choose one that you like. Don't get too cute (don't use phrases like "Expectantly yours" for example). Remember that this is a business transaction.

"ELECTRONIC COVER LETTERS"

FAX. The cover letter that accompanies a faxed resume can follow all of the rules above. In fact, there does not need to be any difference between a faxed cover letter and one sent by conventional mail or overnight express.

However, it is highly recommended that you mail a copy of any resume that you have faxed, for reasons made clear in earlier discussions of photocopying and scanning. When you do send an "original" paper copy of your resume, it should be accompanied by a cover letter. It can either be the identical cover letter that you sent along with the fax or it can note at the beginning that it is a paper copy that is being sent after the faxed copy.

Don't just stick a resume into an envelope and send it after you have faxed it. Always be sure to send a cover letter along with it.

E-MAIL. If you are transmitting your resume by electronic mail, it still needs a cover letter. And that cover letter needs to follow the guidelines above. However, the "rules" of e-mail dictate a few modifications of the guidelines.

First, business e-mail correspondence should be kept as brief as possible. Remember that you are intruding on someone's computer time when you send an e-mail message, so you have to get right to the point. This means that you need to strip down the cover letter that you would have sent on paper to its most vital points. The paragraphs outlined in the guidelines remain the same, but each will need to be shorter.

Second, be sure to mention in your cover letter whether you are appending your resume without its formatting codes (see the chapter on printing your resume for more complete information). If you have been asked to send your resume in a format that will be directly entered into a computerized storage system, you may be sending it as "raw text." This won't look good to prospective employers and they should be warned of this.

Note: It is quite possible to send both a formatted and an unformatted resume by e-mail. This allows employers to read the formatted version and forward the unformatted version to the computerized storage system. To learn more about how to do this with your own word processing and e-mail systems, check with computer-literate co-workers, with friends who are "into computers," or with a local computer store.

Finally, remember that sending your resume by e-mail does not mean that you are suddenly a buddy of the prospective employer at the receiving end of your e-mail. You may have developed many e-mail relationships with many on-line friends and you may "chat" regularly with dozens of people at computers around the world, but you can't "chat" with a potential employer. E-mail among friends (and even around office networks) is often quite casual. Rules of grammar, spelling, and punctuation are often ignored or seriously bent. But all of the "old" rules still apply when you e-mail a cover letter and resume.

Proofread your e-mail cover letter just as carefully as you would if you were putting it into conventional mail. If your e-mail system has a "spell checker," use it. Subject your cover letter to every one of the tests that you would give it before you put it into an envelope.

A SPECIAL NOTE ON "SALARY HISTORY"

There is one request that is frequently made by employers in advertised openings that you DON'T have to address directly in your cover letters. This is the request for your "salary requirements" or for a "salary history." Unless you have very firm salary demands—so firm that you are willing to take yourself out of the running for a position even before you receive an interview—you should not name a precise dollar figure in your cover letter. Don't state exactly what you earn now and don't state what you expect your next job to pay.

Let's face it. There are many more factors to a job than salary alone. There may be a great benefits package to consider. Maybe the opportunities for advancement are tremendous. Or perhaps you're desperate for a job and would work for almost anything. Whatever your personal situation, the salary question is one that should be answered vaguely. It is perfectly acceptable to include a statement like: "My salary requirements are flexible." You might follow that with: "I will be happy to discuss them in an interview."

Even if you are sure that you know what the salary is when you are applying for a job, being vague in your cover letter can still pay off for you. Most jobs have salary ranges attached to them instead of one specific figure. You don't want to state an amount at the low end of the range because that is what you are likely to be offered if you get the job. At the same time, you don't want to give a figure at the high end of the range because you may be seen as greedy or out of the reach of the employer.

If you have a specific salary in mind, it is still best not to be too direct. For example, if you are making $34,000 per year now, you might say in your cover letter: "I expect that the position will offer a salary in the high 30's." Even if you know that the salary has a wide range, don't request a range yourself. (Don't write "I am looking for a job that pays in the mid to high 30's," because you are bound to be offered a salary at the low end of your own stated range.) Notice, too, in our example that the expectation was stated in terms of what the position might pay and not in what the job seeker was demanding. Although employers believe that they want to hear the salary requirements of applicants, they often discriminate against candidates who directly state salary demands in their cover letters.

If you find yourself responding to a job advertisement that includes a statement like "Resumes without salary requirements will not be considered," you still have a couple of choices. You can follow the example above and state: "My salary requirements are flexible, but I expect that the position will offer a salary in the high 30's"; or you can state a minimum: "I expect that the salary will be

at least $35,000 a year." Employers often include this requirement in their ads when a job is paying far less that most employees would expect to receive, so be forewarned.

On the next page you will find a checklist to use in evaluating your cover letter. It restates the advice offered above in the form of questions. Read it now and then read it again after you have drafted a letter of your own. After the checklist there are several sample cover letters. None of these will be exactly right for your situation but you should be able to get direction and inspiration here for writing your own cover letters. Look them over and start writing. It's not nearly as hard as you think.

Use the checklist to critique your cover letters. If you can answer "yes" to every question, you have an excellent cover letter—and an excellent chance of getting an interview. If you can't answer "yes" to every question, go back and make some changes to your letter.

Remember that a good cover letter can persuade an employer to read your resume and a really good cover letter can prepare an employer to like your resume even before it's been read!

COVER LETTER CHECKLIST

1. Is your cover letter addressed to a specific person? (Are you sure that this is the correct person and that you have spelled the name and the title correctly? Do you have the address correct, both mail and e-mail?)

2. Does your cover letter state clearly why you are writing?

3. Does it tell the employer why you are qualified for the position you are seeking? Does it provide examples of your qualifications?

4. Does it tell an employer what you can contribute to the organization? Do you include accomplishments or personal qualifications that suggest the contributions you can make?

5. Does it highlight the most relevant facts about you and your background? Do you connect those facts directly to the needs of the employer?

6. Does it use "action words" to describe your accomplishments, skills, qualifications and experience?

7. Does it respond directly to an ad or job description? Do you address each of the points mentioned in the ad or description?

8. Does it avoid "jargon" that might not be understood by the recipient?

9. Is it persuasive? Does it encourage the reader to read the accompanying resume?

10. Does it avoid negative statements and apologies?

11. Have you cut out anything that seems vague or insincere?

12. Are the paragraphs short (no more than five lines each)?

13. Does it fit neatly onto one page (or less if it will be sent by electronic mail)?

14. Is it well typed and attractively presented?

15. Does it include your name, address, and phone number?

16. Does it explain how to contact you to set up an interview?

17. Does it state what you expect to happen next? (Are you going to wait for a call? Are you going to call to follow up? When are you going to call?)

18. Is it grammatically correct?

19. Is everything spelled correctly?

20. Have you had a friend or colleague read it and offer an opinion?

CONGRATULATIONS! If you can answer "yes" to these questions, you have done a terrific job on your cover letter—and it's ready to send!

1339 Longwood Ave.
Brookline, MA 02146

May 16, 1996

Ms. Lorraine Chu
Vice-President, Finance
Software Solutions, Inc.
210 Federal St.
Boston, MA 02063

Dear Ms. Chu:

I am responding to your advertisement in the *Boston Globe* for an Accounts Payable Supervisor. My experience has prepared me well for this position and I believe that I can make a significant contribution to your department and to your company.

As you will see on my enclosed resume, I am currently Accounts Payable Supervisor at Data General. Immediately after I was hired I was closely involved in the consolidation and reorganization of the accounting department. We were able to increase our operating efficiencies and decrease our expenditures, resulting in a savings to the company of more than $100,000 per year. Although my specific area lost two full-time staff members, we were actually able to process payments in less time than we had before the reorganization. I have been an active member of the departmental management team and I believe that my experience and enthusiasm will be directly transferable to Software Solutions.

I would like to meet with you in person to discuss the position and my background. I look forward to receiving a call from you to set up a time to meet. If I don't hear from you by the end of May I will give you a call then. Thank you for your time and consideration.

Sincerely,

Catherine McDaniel

June 21, 1996

Mr. John Shearing
Director of Human Resources
Bristol-Myers-Squibb
Province Line Road
Princeton, NJ 08540

Dear Mr. Shearing:

Through my university's Office of Career Planning and Placement, I have learned that you have an opening for a Manager of Corporate Fitness Programs. I have just graduated from Wayne State University with a degree in Corporate Fitness and I believe that I am well qualified to lead this department at your firm. As you may know, Wayne State was one of the first universities to establish degree programs in Corporate Fitness and I have both a strong academic background and a substantial amount of relevant work experience.

As my resume details, I have already held positions as Fitness Center Supervisor at NCR Corporation, Fitness Assistant at a leading corporate fitness consulting firm, and Cardiac Rehabilitation Assistant at a major medical center. These experiences, combined with my classroom preparation, have provided me with the skills to step directly into the position that you have advertised. From the placement office, I learned that this position has only been in existence for two years and that you are looking for someone who can continue to expand and improve the program. That is exactly the kind of challenge I'm seeking.

I look forward to the chance to discuss the position with you. Although I do not live in New Jersey, I am available to interview at any time and on short notice. I hope to hear from you in the near future. Thank you for your consideration.

Sincerely,

Jason Harris
812 Jefferson St.
New Haven, IN 46774

July 22, 1996

Richard Ramirez
Staff Recruiter
Office of Human Resources
Grumman Aviation
17829 Coast Highway
Redondo Beach, CA 93602

Dear Mr. Ramirez:

I am writing to you at the suggestion of Edward Thieu, who is employed in your new-product engineering department. He thinks that my experiences and skills would be an asset to Grumman and I hope that I can explore employment opportunities with you at the end of the summer.

I am presently an Assistant Air Department Officer at the Naval Air Warfare Center in Honolulu. I expect to receive my honorable discharge from the Navy at the end of August and I will be returning to Southern California at that time. My experiences in the armed forces are directly relevant to Grumman Aviation. As you will see on the resume I have enclosed, much of my military career has involved administration of large-scale operations. Currently I supervise 25 air traffic controllers, 15 equipment maintenance technicians, and 10 aircraft line handlers. In less than five years I have contributed to reducing the cost of aircraft maintenance by 25% and have overseen a reduction in staffing of 35%. I have personally supervised the transition of my department to a new computer system, running two systems in parallel for six months.

I believe that these skills could be of immediate benefit to Grumman. I would like to meet with you in early September to discuss the ways in which I can make a contribution to your organization. I will call you in mid-August to set up an appointment. Even if you don't have a specific job opening or a position in mind, I do think that it will be worthwhile to meet. I will speak with you soon.

Cordially,

William Newkirk
87342 Mokauea Ave., Apt.44
Honolulu, HI 96816

"I'm putting your resume on top of the pile where I'll be sure to see it."

CHAPTER 24

SAMPLE RESUMES

A WEALTH OF POSSIBILTIES

On the pages that follow you will find a number of state-of-the-art resumes. As you look through these sample resumes, don't restrict yourself to studying only those in your own occupational field. Be sure to take a look at each resume. There is much in these samples that can benefit you as you prepare your own resume.

In addition to studying what is contained in the resumes, notice what's missing. Because electronic scanners are programmed only to "read" words, they are confused by many of the devices that resumes once contained, like "bullets," asterisks, underlining, bordering lines, etc. This poses a challenge for anyone writing a resume today: how can a resume look appealing to people and to computers alike? All of the resumes that follow have met that challenge. They offer a wealth of possibilities. Below are a few suggestions on how you might use the samples.

1) Organization. See how each resume is organized. Notice how the most important information is near the top of the resume. Because each person's "selling points" are different, it follows that each resume has a different organization.

2) Design. There are many ways to create a "look" for a resume. You may immediately like the look of one of the samples; you may want to blend elements of several samples into your own resume; or you may decide to create a new design of your own.

3) Phrasing. Spend some time actually reading the sample resumes. Each has been carefully worded. Look especially at the phrasing of skills, accomplishments, and personal qualifications. These may be useful in writing your own resume.

4) Occupations. It's not true that all resumes in a certain occupation should look alike. In fact, you want your resume to stand out from others. However, if there are samples in your occupational area, take a close look at how these writers have presented themselves.

5) Problems. Everyone who writes a resume faces some special problems. Perhaps some of the problems you face were overcome in the resumes that follow. Remember to check the notes at the bottom of each resume, since they often point out solutions to specific problems.

Lucinda Cree

8080 Humphrey Way
Arlington, VA 22205
(703) 975-2804
Email: lcree@nmu.com

PROFILE   Computer systems generalist with specialties in medical insurance and malpractice insurance.

ACCOMPLISHMENTS

- Worked with both internal and external customers to implement, develop and refine a medical malpractice policy rating, billing and collection system for 8,000 policies totaling $100 million in premiums
- Installed database system in 3 outside medical malpractice insurance companies providing ongoing service to external and internal customers
- Expanded the policy services system to include issuance and billing of corporate policies numbering more than 4,500
- Designed and oversaw development of system for tracking commissions payable to brokers, reducing expenses by more than 20%
- Worked closely with finance to ensure timely and accurate accounts receivable, resulting in reducing average collection time by 15 days

SKILLS

- Knowledge of Unix operating system
- Comprehension of DOS, Word Perfect 5.0, Lotus 1-2-3 on PC-based platform
- Knowledge of programming languages: C and COBOL
- Strong oral and written communications skills
- Excellent administrative and supervisory skills

EMPLOYMENT

<u>Supervisor</u>, Department of Information, National Medical Underwriters, Alexandria, VA

<u>Customer Service Liaison</u>, National Medical Underwriters

EDUCATION

B.S., Biology, University of Virginia

Continuing Education courses in Management Information Systems, Department of Electrical Engineering and Computer Systems at George Washington University

Note: This is Lucinda's "print" resume. Her "electronic" resume is on the facing page. Note the differences in its design!

Lucinda Cree

8080 Humphrey Way
Arlington, VA 22205
(703) 975-2804
Email: lcree@nmu.com

PROFILE   Computer systems generalist with specialties in medical insurance and malpractice insurance.

ACCOMPLISHMENTS

Worked with both internal and external customers to implement, develop and refine a medical malpractice policy rating, billing and collection system for 8,000 policies totaling $100 million in premiums

Installed database system in 3 outside medical malpractice insurance companies providing ongoing service to external and internal customers

Expanded the policy services system to include issuance and billing of corporate policies numbering more than 4,500

Designed and oversaw development of system for tracking commissions payable to brokers, reducing expenses by more than 20%

Worked closely with finance to ensure timely and accurate accounts receivable, resulting in reducing average collection time by 15 days

SKILLS

Knowledge of Unix operating system
Comprehension of DOS, Word Perfect 5.0, Lotus 1-2-3 on PC-based platform
Knowledge of programming languages: C and COBOL
Strong oral and written communications skills
Excellent administrative and supervisory skills

EMPLOYMENT

SUPERVISOR, Department of Information, National Medical Underwriters, Alexandria, VA

CUSTOMER SERVICE LIAISON, National Medical Underwriters

EDUCATION

B.S., Biology, University of Virginia

Continuing Education courses in Management Information Systems, Department of Electrical Engineering and Computer Systems at George Washington University

Note: Lucinda's "electronic" resume clearly highlights her accomplishments and skills. She does not include the customary "experience" section.

WESLEY JOHNSON

382 Shady Point Drive
Broken Arrow, OK 74728
918-161-0842

JOURNEYMAN ELECTRICIAN

Highly skilled, meticulous, efficient, dependable worker,
with experience in industry and private contracting.

Education/Licenses
- ✓ State of Oklahoma Electrical Contractor License
- ✓ Completed 4-year Journeyman Electrician Apprenticeship Training Course
- ✓ Relevant Coursework:
  - -Electromagnetic Fundamentals
  - -AC Theory & Circuit Characteristics
  - -Residential/Commercial/Industrial Wiring
  - -Circuit Concepts
  - -Lighting Systems
  - -AC & DC Motors/Machinery and Controls
  - -Three-Phase Alternators/Transformers
  - -Polyphase Circuits

Experience

Electrician, E-Z Glide Transport Systems, Tulsa, OK
- Construct, install and repair a wide variety of electrical, electronic and mechanical systems, including commercial lighting, motor controls, wiring installations, control wiring for machinery fabricated on the premises (conveyor systems and specialized equipment).
- Install and repair HVAC equipment, boiler systems, circulator pumps, electric valve systems; hydraulic system maintenance and repair. (1994–present)

Electrician, Ace Electrical Contracting, Tulsa, OK
- Construction, repair and troubleshooting of commercial and residential electrical systems.
- Completed wiring of light commercial buildings and warehouses, strip stores, fire detector circuits, phone installations, underground feeder circuits and custom lighting. (1991–94)

Related Interests
- Member of Rail Ravers, a model train club that has 200-square-foot layout at the Children's Hospital of Tulsa. Donate approximately 8 hours per month to repairing, troubleshooting and expanding the system.

Note: Wesley's "print" resume is not designed for computer scanning. See his "electronic" resume on the next page.

Wesley Johnson

382 Shady Point Drive
Broken Arrow, OK 74728
918-161-0842

JOURNEYMAN ELECTRICIAN

Highly skilled, meticulous, efficient, dependable worker, with experience
in industry and private contracting.

Education/Licenses

State of Oklahoma Electrical Contractor License
Completed 4-year Journeyman Electrician Apprenticeship Training Course
Relevant Coursework:

Electromagnetic Fundamentals	Lighting Systems
AC Theory & Circuit Characteristics	Circuit Concepts
Residential/Commercial/Industrial Wiring	Three-Phase Alternators/Transformers
AC & DC Motors/Machinery and Controls	Polyphase Circuits

Experience

Electrician, E-Z Glide Transport Systems, Tulsa, OK (1994–present)
Construct, install and repair a wide variety of electrical, electronic and
mechanical systems, including commercial lighting, motor controls, wiring
installations, control wiring for machinery fabricated on the premises
(conveyor systems and specialized equipment).

Install and repair HVAC equipment, boiler systems, circulator pumps,
electric valve systems; hydraulic system maintenance and repair.

Electrician, Ace Electrical Contracting, Tulsa, OK (1991–94)
Construction, repair and troubleshooting of commercial and residential
electrical systems.

Completed wiring of light commercial buildings and warehouses, strip stores,
fire detector circuits, phone installations, underground feeder circuits and
custom lighting.

Related Interests

Member of Rail Ravers, a model train club that has 200-square-foot layout at
the Children's Hospital of Tulsa. Donate approximately 8 hours per month
to repairing, troubleshooting and expanding the system.

*Note: Wesley's "electronic" resume is set up for scanning. Because education and
licensing are important in his field, he puts these near the top, just below a
"qualifications" statement.*

Charlotte Schultz

8293 West Mountain Drive
Alexander, Arkansas 72202
(501) 993-3420

OBJECTIVE   Hard-working college graduate with degree in accounting wants to make a contribution to the financial health of a bank or business.

EXPERIENCE
LITTLE ROCK SAVINGS BANK, Little Rock, AR
Bank Reconciliation Technician 6/92 - present
Reconcile investor custodial accounts
Research inquiries from mortgagors and investors regarding disbursements
Initiate wire transfer of funds between savings bank and Federal Home Loan Bank
Investigate foreclosure loss at loan level basis, enabling management to make
  proper account entry decisions

Cash Technician (part-time position) 1/91-6/92
Reconciled foreclosure loss reserve accounts
Prepared Real Estate Owned reports for presentation to Board of Directors
Processed payoffs, regular installment payments and foreclosure settlements

UNIVERSITY OF ARKANSAS, Little Rock, AR 6/89-9/89
Bookkeeper, Council of Student Organizations
Paid part-time accounting position
Dispersed more than $500,000 in student funds
Wrote all checks requested by more than 75 student organizations

EDUCATION
University of Arkansas, Little Rock, AR
Degree: Bachelor of Science, June 1992
Major: Accounting   G.P.A.: 3.56   (on a 4.0 scale)
Note: Self-financed 80% of cost of education

SKILLS
Lotus 1-2-3; Quattro; Paradox; Data Base 111; Wordstar: Professional Write

ACTIVITIES
National Association of Accountants (Student Member) 1990-1992
Delta Delta Delta Sorority 1989-1992, Treasurer 1991-1992

REFERENCES
Available upon request

Note: Charlotte makes the most of her limited experience and keeps the resume focused on accounting and finance. Notice her treatment of part-time work.

Andrea Summerson
815 Carroll Way
Juneau, AK 99801
(907) 442-9067

SUMMARY
Over 5 years experience installing, troubleshooting, administering, developing, implementing and training with IBM/PC's in a Local Area Network Token Ring Architecture and with Wang's PC's in a Wide Area Network

ACCOMPLISHMENTS
ADMINISTRATION
Administered, planned and maintained a Local Area Network made up of
        IBM PS/2's on an OS/2 Token Ring
In charge of distributing and maintaining all computer equipment for office
Delivered, installed, and provided maintenance on networked PC's, mainframes,
        and software for 120 legislative district offices, eliminating
        the need for a $250K maintenance contract

DEVELOPMENT
Developed interface between Auditor's office PC LAN and the Legislature's
        Bill Tracking and Statute Retrieval System, improving auditor efficiency
Developed and implemented an inventory and resume database used by
        peer review for annual certification
Improved productivity by developing and implementing a project
        management system

TECHNICAL
Hardware   Token Ring LAN Architecture using IBM PS/2's, Wang Systems
Software   WordPerfect, Multimate, Quattro Pro, E-Mail,
                Lotus 1-2-3, dBase, Alpha 4, SAS
Operating
Systems   OS/2, MS-DOS, JCL

EXPERIENCE
State of Alaska, State Auditor's Office, Juneau, AK
        Auditor, 12/92 - Present
State of Alaska, Office of Legislative Services, Juneau, AK
        PC User Consultant, 7/89 - 12/92

EDUCATION
University of Alaska, Juneau, AK
BS in Business Administration, Major: Accounting, 1989 - 1992
Sheldon Jackson College, Sitka, AK 1988 - 1989

Note: Andrea divides her accomplishments into three separate categories and then lists her employment history under the heading of "Experience."

EUGENE HERR
80-B Glendale Ave.
Lanham, MD 20706
(410) 608-3380

OBJECTIVE: Seeking responsible position in corporate security.
Offering extensive experience and education.

EXPERIENCE:
Senior Correction Officer, Maryland State Correctional Facility (1995-present)
Control Post Officer with detail of approximately 30 officers, overseeing access to four
major areas
Procure supplies, issue job assignments and supervise inmate workers in their
assigned tasks
Maintain monthly payroll and rating system for employees, including weekly updates
Perform various other custody functions including inmate and area searches,
maintaining discipline, and control of contraband
Perform investigations on inmate infractions and issue disciplinary reports
Supervise up to three officers in conducting investigations

Senior Correction Officer, Baltimore County Youth Home (1987-1989)
Housing Officer in charge of approximately 20 juveniles on an assigned shift
Maintained custody and control of juveniles while also safeguarding their well-being
and attending to their individual needs

EDUCATION:
Pursuing B.S. in Administration of Justice, Bowie State College
Degree expected, June 1996
A.A.S., Corrections, Community College of Baltimore, 1990

MILITARY:
Operations Officer, U.S. Army, Berlin, Germany (1992-1995)
Responsible for developing, producing, acquiring and supporting weapons systems,
ammunition, missiles and ground mobility material during peace and war
Comprehensive knowledge of maintenance management, production control and
quality assurance

Officer Candidate School, Quantico, VA
Commissioned Officer, 2nd Lieutenant, September 1, 1992

REFERENCES: Excellent personal and professional references available upon request.

PLEASE MAINTAIN THE CONFIDENTIALITY OF THIS RESUME

Note: Eugene's military service comes between his two jobs but he groups the related
work together and handles military service in its own section.

ALICE KATSOURIS

1063 Mansfield Ave.
Melrose Park, IL 60164
(312) 785-3043 (Office)
(312) 865-6302 (Home)

SUMMARY

Award-winning copywriter
> Work effectively as team member
> Relate well to clients
> Skilled in research techniques
> Manage photographers, graphic designers, media planners, and
>> production personnel
> Develop effective advertising, marketing, and p.r. campaigns

EXPERIENCE

General Foods (print ads) Pioneer Audio (package design) Westside Electronics (newspaper ads) Mita Copiers (collateral materials) Chicago City College (magazine, newspaper, transit ads) Chicago Museum of Art (direct mail campaign awarded first place in competition with all museums in Illinois)

EMPLOYMENT

Megacom (ad agency) Chicago, IL
> Senior copywriter
Smith, Coverdale (ad agency) Chicago, IL
> Copywriter
Clovis and Maven (ad agency) Chicago, IL
> Copywriter

EDUCATION

B.A., English, Lake Forest College, Lake Forest, IL
Participant, "Shakespeare Semester," Stratford-on-Avon, England

PERSONAL

Volunteer Director, Southside Children's Theater, Chicago
Drama coach/director at inner city theater program for disadvantaged youth

Note: Advertising-industry resumes concentrate on accounts and campaigns. Their design can be flamboyant. Dates are not essential.

MADELINE MORALES

c/o Griffin Talent Management
11925 Peachtree Road
Atlanta, GA 30318
(404) 977-3422

TELEVISION: "Days of Our Lives": Waitress (speaking part)
"Santa Barbara": Nurse (walk-on)
"Beverly Hills 90210": Secretary (non-speaking)

NATIONAL ADVERTISING: Atlanta Braves: Fan (close-up)
Georgia Tourism Board: Vendor (speaking)

LOCAL ADVERTISING: 15 appearances to date including 10 speaking parts.
Featured parts in commercials for Peachtree Spa,
Doubletree Hotels, and Calhoun Nissan.

NATIONAL FILM: "Doc Hollywood": patient (non-speaking)
"My Cousin Vinny": courtroom spectator (non-speaking)

VIDEO: 21 appearances to date in industrial videos. Featured
parts in 5 videos, including narrator for "Our Georgia:
Welcome To It" produced for GeorgiaTourism Board
(on-screen speaking and overdubbed narration).

TALENTS: Read and speak Spanish.
Excellent with accents. Can do inflected English, with
Spanish, French, and Italian accents.
Face and hands used extensively in close-ups.
Can portray numerous ethnicities.
Good with children of all ages.
Good with all kinds of animals.
Play piano, flute, violin, viola.

Note: Can travel. Available on short notice.

Note: This is a typical resume for an actress. It will be sent with a photo. If this resume is "scanned" electronically, a human "verifier" will check the spelling of the name.

CURRICULUM VITAE

DEBORAH HAMILTON
University of Oklahoma, Department of English
Norman, OK 73019
(405) 878-0845
Email:dhamilton@oklahoma.edu

PRESENT POSITION
Assistant Professor of English, University of Missouri, 1994 - Present

EDUCATION
Ph.D., English, University of Georgia, Athens, GA 1991
>   Dissertation: "The Dark Side of The Moonstone: Tragedy and Melodrama
>   in the Works of Wilkie Collins"

M.A., English, University of Georgia 1989
B.A., English, Spelman College, Atlanta, GA 1985
>   Graduated with honors
>   Distinction in senior thesis

TEACHING EXPERIENCE
Visiting Adjunct Instructor of English, Georgia Southwestern College,
>   Americus, GA 1992 - 94

Courses included: Composition 1, Introduction to English Literature, Introduction to the
>   Victorian Novel

Teaching Assistant, University of Georgia, 1987 - 92
Courses included: Composition, Advanced Composition, Honors Composition,
>   Introduction to Literature, English Literature: An Introduction,
>   The Victorians, Introduction to the Victorian Novel

ADMINISTRATIVE EXPERIENCE
Coordinator, Freshman Composition Program, University of Georgia 1990 - 92
Elected representative to faculty senate, Graduate Student Association, 1989

PUBLICATIONS
"The Dark Side of The Moonstone: Tragedy and Melodrama in the Works of
>   Wilkie Collins," accepted for editorial review by University of California Press and
>   University of Chicago Press

"Tragedy Meets Melodrama: Wilkie Collins and The Moonstone,"
>   "19th-Century Literature," Vol. 10, 2, Summer 1995

"Melodrama and Tragedy in Victorian Novels," published as chapter in
>   "Teaching the Victorian Novel" (University of Minnesota Press, 1994)

LANGUAGES
French: reading proficiency, writing proficiency, speaking fluency
German: reading proficiency   Spanish: speaking proficiency

Note: This is a "vita." Deborah is typical of a professor early in a career.
The section entitled "Administrative Experience" is a smart addition to the vita.

PETER HANRATTY

120 Spur Circle
Houston, TX 77020
(713) 592-2312
(713) 579-1340 (pager)

SUMMARY

Offering over 12 years' experience in the Information Systems and Telecommunications industry: 5 years in technical training and 7 years directly dealing with customer support and equipment maintenance

QUALIFICATIONS

Skilled teacher
Experienced engineer
Effective with clients, coworkers, and computers
Thorough knowledge of UNISYS product line
Productive in a variety of work settings

ACCOMPLISHMENTS

UNISYS CORPORATION, HOUSTON, TX

Developer / Instructor (1988–present)
Responsible for the development and delivery of training for PC and Unix communications and network products
Led team to develop a self-paced computer-, video- and text-based training package which was accepted as corporate standard and used nationwide
Developed and conducted more than 20 hardware classes on mainframes, mini's and PC's
Developed and conducted more than 10 software classes on operating systems and applications

Senior Site Engineer (1981–1988)
Responsible for installation, maintenance, upgrade and repair for mainframes, peripherals and communications equipment. Increased installation efficiency by 15%, leading to improved customer satisfaction and decreased company costs.
Employed preventative maintenance procedures to maintain on-line site efficiency of 99.5%. This resulted in one of the lowest "down time" rates of any corporate field office.

PLEASE SEE NEXT PAGE

PETER HANRATTY
Page Two

MILITARY SERVICE

U.S. AIR FORCE (1973-1981)
Responsibilities included maintenance and repair of
airfield-based and mobile communications, radar
and navigational equipment

EDUCATION

U.S. AIR FORCE Technical Training School
Associate Degree
Note: Earned A.A.S. degree while enlisted.
Emphasis on computer systems design and
maintenance.

TECHNICAL TRAINING

UNISYS Education Center, Houston, TX
UNIX Communications & Networking, 1992
UNIX Shell Programming, 1992
UNIX System Administration, 1992
Local Area Network Administration, 1990
1100/90 Advanced Troubleshooting, 1989
110/60 System Maintenance, 1988
Peripheral Theory & Repair, 1987
U1050 - II System Maintenance, 1985

SOFTWARE EXPERIENCE

LAN   Novell Netware 286
UNIX   System V.3, Shell, C, TCP/IP, UUCP, FTP, SMTP
PC   MS-DOS, Basic, C, dBase III, Clipper, Excell 2.1,
Word Perfect 5.1, Draw Perfect 1.1, Harvard Graphics
2.1, XyWrite III, Misc Utilities
Mainframe OS11OO, ECL

HARDWARE EXPERIENCE

PC Unisys - HT, JT, UIT, PW2 500
Communication Unisys - DCP40/20/10
Mainframe Unisys- 2200/600ES, 2200/600, 2200/400,
2200/200, 100/90, System II/Mapper 10, 1100/60,1050-II
Peripheral Unisys - Disk: 8433, 8436, 8440, 8451, 8470
Unisys - Tape: U22/24, U26/28, U30/32, Steamer
Unisys - Printer: 770-II, 776, 789

*Note: Peter's resume is well-detailed and very specific. He devotes the first page
to catching attention and the second to technical specifications.*

JEANETTE JOHNS
52314 Red Hill Avenue
Tustin, California 92705
Home (714) 838-6807
Work (714) 749-3829

PROFESSIONAL OBJECTIVE
Position as a Learning Disability Teacher/Consultant

HIGHLIGHTS OF QUALIFICATIONS
Over 15 years experience meeting educational needs of special students
Committed to equal opportunities for all students
Capable of working in varied settings
Collaborate well with colleagues and administration

PROFESSIONAL EXPERIENCE

ASSESSMENT
Evaluated students using varied assessment methods including:
- standardized and criterion instruments
- curriculum-based assessment
- diagnostic teaching
- student and teacher interview
- record review and classroom observation

Assessed students presenting a diversity of educationally handicapping conditions including emotional disturbance, all levels of retardation, autism, multiple handicaps and learning difficulties.

COLLABORATIVE PROBLEM SOLVING
Empowered teachers to develop more effective instruction to meet the needs of an extremely diverse student population.
Obtained support and involvement from administrative, professional and non-professional staff to identify and address instructional challenges.

CASE MANAGEMENT
Performed approximately 100 annual reviews and reclassifications in compliance with state and federal regulations.

CURRICULUM DEVELOPMENT
Assisted in the development of a Curriculum Guide used in the educational facilities of the Department of Human Services.
Researched and wrote curriculum for mental health course used with students in a psychiatric facility. Course spanned 3 years and involved 300 participants. Program was submitted by Department of Human Services to the American Psychiatric Association's Achievement Awards Competition.

(CONTINUED)

JEANETTE JOHNS
Page 2

WORK EXPERIENCE

Learning Disability Teacher/Consultant, 1992 - Present
  Serve as case manager for Douglas Training and Research Center and Naremore
    Development Center
  Perform educational assessment for 8 local inpatient and outpatient psychiatric centers
  Conduct per-case evaluations for private, public and parochial schools

Teacher, Frederick Psychiatric Hospital, 1984 - 1992
  Full-time position working with students of all ages and backgrounds
  Implemented innovative peer reading program

Teacher, Special Education - various public school districts, 1977 - 1984
  Experienced in T.M.R., Resource Room and Primary ED class
  Supervised para-professional assistants
  Developed reading programs

PROFESSIONAL CERTIFICATIONS
L.D.T.C. 1990
Teacher of the Handicapped 1977
Elementary Education 1977

EDUCATION
1990 University of Southern California, L.D.T.C. Certification Program
1988 University of Southern California - Course leading to Principal Certification
1982 M.A., University of Southern California, Special Education
1977 B.A., California State College, Fullerton, Major - English, Minor - Elementary Education

PROFESSIONAL ASSOCIATIONS
California Association for Learning Consultants
Council for Exceptional Children

REFERENCES
Will be furnished upon request

Note: Jeanette first highlights her qualifications and experience and then details her employment and education. Observe the "keywords" in Assessment section.

MANGIT GULERIA

437 Canal St. #7
New York, NY 10013
(212) 868-1562

QUALIFICATIONS

Graphic artist skilled in the use of state-of-the-art technologies
Electronically "draw" images for computer animation
Create special effects in type and backgrounds for a nationally televised
home shopping service
Design storyboards on computer
Shoot, edit, and sound-edit short video footage
Utilize all traditional graphic arts in design of print materials

EXPERIENCE

Video Layout Artist, Electronic Media Department, Macy's, Inc.,
New York, NY (1993 - Present)
Computer graphic artist for televised home shopping service
Create still video screens (with type and images) for national broadcast
Develop and implement procedures, techniques, and formats for adapting
color catalog ektachromes to television medium
Interact with printed catalog art staff as liaison from electronic
catalog department

Senior Graphic Artist, Consumer Catalog Department, Macy's, Inc.,
New York, NY (1990 - 1993)
Supervising layout artist for 4 major catalogs and 28 tabloids per year
Designed layout and type specifications
Interfaced with photographers and printers to ensure accurate and
timely production of catalogs
Created new design formats for publication

TECHNICAL

Skilled in use of Macintosh computers and peripherals
Skilled in use of numerous design software packages, including PageMaker,
Studio 8, Quark Xpress, MacroMind Director, Type Styler and others
Skilled in use of Colorgraphics Art Star 3D computer and peripherals

EDUCATION

B.A., Fine Arts, New York University
Continuing education courses at Parsons Institute of Design, New York City

Note: Mangit positions herself immediately with her qualifications. She has been a graphic artist for many years but she does not indicate any dates that might reveal her age.

GEORGE MARION
1072 Delmar Avenue
Pismo Beach, CA 93449
(707) 857-38123
E-mail: gmarion@allcraft.com

SUMMARY **Marketing Manager skilled in all phases of marketing, with special strengths in catalog marketing and targeted direct-response marketing.**

EXPERIENCE **Marketing Manager**, Allcraft Publishing, San Luis Obispo, CA
Increased sales volume by 15% in first year
Reduced marketing expenses by 20% in first year
   through better targeting of catalog mailing
Increased catalog sales by 30% in three years
Increased overall response rates from 4% to 8%: a 100% jump in
   three years

Assistant Marketing Manager, Alessi Yarn Co., Los Angeles, CA
Doubled income from direct-to-consumer marketing
Initiated first consumer advertising campaign
Supervised transition from black-and-white to four-color
   catalogs for wholesalers, retailers, and consumers

Assistant Marketing Manager, Wonderland Looms, Duluth, MN

Sales Representative, Wonderland Looms, Duluth, MN

EDUCATION Bachelor of Business Administration
University of Iowa, Iowa City, IA
Major: Marketing   Minor: Advertising

PERSONAL Volunteer tutor at La Raza Community Center,
   San Luis Obispo, CA
Volunteer speaker in local program: "Education Means Jobs"

Note: Willing to relocate. Willing to travel.

Note: As a marketing manager, George concentrates on his tangible results in his two most recent jobs. This attractive resume will "scan" well.

Lisa Redfern

438-D Willow Creek Road
Eagle River, Alaska 99577
(907) 854-2458

PROFILE

Hard working, conscientious Physician Assistant, skilled at putting people at ease and inspiring confidence in the physician, treatment, and the practice

Well-versed in the Managed Health Care environment

Knowledgeable with medical billing and patient management software

Demonstrated leader as well as team member

Able to function under stress and within short time frames

EXPERIENCE

Physician Assistant

Lisa Gaffney, M.D., Anchorage, Alaska

Takes medical history and performs physical examinations for a family practice in internal medicine with over 8000 active files

Treats acerations, abrasions and burns

Makes preliminary diagnoses, carries out appropriate treatment, performs phlebotomy and orders required lab tests

Answers questions about treatments and procedures in order to put patients at ease

Assists with minor in-office surgery, OB-GYN examinations, performs cardiograms and administers immunizations

Performs chemistries with biodynamics reagents using spectrometrics methods

Handles insurance billing using Signature software

Pays bills, orders supplies and maintains records

Physician Assistant to Dermatologist (Part Time)

Providence Hospital, Anchorage, Alaska

Screened calls in order to determine severity and scheduled appointments depending on need

Assisted the Dermatologist within a Managed Health Care environment

Conferred with patients, answered inquiries and provided information over the telephone

EDUCATION

University of Alaska, Anchorage, Alaska
Physician Assistant Program
Licensed as Physician Assistant

University of Alaska, Fairbanks, Alaska
B.S., Biology

City University of New York
Elementary Education and Biology

Note: Lisa describes herself in the "Profile" section in a way that will make a prospective employer keep reading. She knows what employers need and she speaks directly to their needs. Her resume includes numerous "keywords."

Alonia Taylor

47 Lawrence Landing
Oxford, MS 38655
(601) 866-2558

OBJECTIVE

A Social Services position in which I can apply counseling, administrative
and communications skills.

COUNSELING

Counseled adolescents with behavioral problems, helping them change their behaviors
Tutored and conducted workshops to improve academic performance of clients
Counseled adolescents in alcohol and drug related matters

CASE MANAGEMENT

Assessed the needs of clients using patience and the process of "talking to, not at"
Put together the most appropriate package of services in consultation with client and
    providers
Followed through with providers to assure that the needed services were delivered

ADMINISTRATION

Assisted in processing applications for naturaliation including fingerprinting,
    photographing, and verifying client information
Handled payments and maintained accounts
Implemented civil rights policies throughout organization

COMMUNICATIONS

Listened to concerns of clients, creating a climate of openness and trust to develop
    solutions
Assisted in writing civil rights guidelines in compliance with federal regulations
Responded to inquiries regarding immigration issues from clients; drafted letters and
    forms

EDUCATION

Jackson State University, Jackson, MS   May 1995
B.A. Degree in Sociology with a Criminal Justice/Juvenile Delinquency concentration

EXPERIENCE

Currently employed at University of Mississippi Office of the General Counsel, Oxford, MS,
6/95-present

Intern - Jackson Police Department, Jackson, MS, 1/95-5/95
Program Specialist - United States Department of Agriculture, Jackson, MS,
    Summer 1994
Legal Assistant - Immigration Law Center, Jackson, MS, Summers 1991 & 1992

*Note: Alonia is not satisfied with her first job after college. She has created a resume
that presents her skills in four specific areas. The "Experience" section is really a
listing of her previous jobs, both paid and unpaid.*

Violet Jenkins
434 NEWFIELD STREET
SOUTH WINDSOR, CT 06074
203-471-0256

PROFILE   Proven ability in processing medical, disability and death claims for an insurance carrier with a local and national client base

WORK EXPERIENCE

PRUDENTIAL INSURANCE CO., INC., Hartford, CT
Claims Processor   10/92-present
Description: Responsible for confirming eligibility of insureds and determining appropriateness of treatment according to terms of the policy

Accomplishments:
Processes 800 claims per month, 25% more than job criteria require
Determines payment criteria in an average of one week, rather than the usual average of two
Recognized by management as an example of outstanding quality-and-service-oriented employee

Responsibilities:
Composes client information, eligibility and collection information on word processor
Obtains required information from doctors, lawyers and hospitals for making eligibility determinations
Processes disability and death claims

File Clerk   10/90-10/92
Description: Duties involved filing and mailing

Responsibilities:
Opened, stamped, and sorted the mail, ensuring proper distribution
Filed mail and documents
Prepared outgoing mail in a timely manner

OLSTEN TEMPORARY SERVICES, Hartford, CT   1/90-10/90
Temporary Employee
Description: Performed a variety of duties, including filing, reception, and word processing

EDUCATION

CENTRAL CONNECTICUT STATE UNIVERSITY, Hartford, CT
Currently enrolled in liberal arts degree program

Note: Violet is a part-time college student and a full-time employee. She nicely includes accomplishments and "facts and figures" in her "Work Experience."

Ada Gonzales
827-B Hunter Terrace
Odessa, TX 79763
(915) 907-4628

OBJECTIVE   A position in law enforcement, investigation, or corporate security. Offering a strong educational background, relevant experience, solid skills, and a commitment to hard work.

EDUCATION

Bachelor of Science (with Honors), May 1995
University of Texas at El Paso
Major: Administration of Justice
Minor: Psychology
Criminology Certificate
GPA: 3.68/4.0

RELEVANT COURSES

Justice in American Society	White-Collar Crime
Court Management and Administration	Criminal Law
Police Organization and Administration	Juvenile Justice
Sociology of Deviant Behavior	Criminology
Principles of Personality	Principles of Abnormal Psychology

INTERNSHIPS

Administration of Justice, El Paso Municipal Court System, Spring 1995
Observation and participation in court system. Averaged 10 hours per week.

Criminology Internship, El Paso Police Department, Fall 1994
Worked in crime investigations unit. Responded to calls and visited crime sites with police officers. Averaged 8 hours per week.

VOLUNTEER EXPERIENCE

Citizen's Advisory Committee, Odessa Police Department, Summers, 1993 and 1994. Served as community representative and liaison with metropolitan police department. Participated in training program for CAC members. Attended more than 20 meetings with community members and police.

ACTIVITIES

Citizens Rifle and Revolver Club, Range Instructor
Junior Rifle Program (P.B.A. sponsored), Range Instructor
Target Shooting, Distinguished Expert Classification
Tang Soo Do Martial Arts

LANGUAGES

Fluent in Spanish and English (written and spoken)

Note: Notice how qualified Ada appears to be for the type of job she wants, even though she has no paid work experience.

Gregory A. Shepherd

3466 Pickwick Circle
Irvington, NE 68152
(402) 708-9345 work
(402) 834-9597 home

SUMMARY

More than 20 years of business experience including total responsibility for operations of companies in Europe as well as Chief Financial Officer for publicly traded company.

EXPERIENCE

T.H. James Systems, Inc., Omaha, NE   6/80-Present
GROUP VICE PRESIDENT, member of Board of Directors and Chief Financial Officer

Responsible for all duties of Chief Financial Officer including S.E.C., Legal, E.D.P., personnel, banking, tax, shareholder relations, and other administrative duties. Operations responsibilities include management of subsidiaries in England, France, and Italy through general managers.

Report to the Chief Executive Officer. Began as Treasurer. Advanced to Vice President of Finance.

Accomplishments:
Involved in overall growth in revenues from $3,000,000 to over $50,000,000
Orchestrated subsidiary turnaround from losing operation to profitable success
Effected spin-off and initial public offering for a subsidiary
Planned public issues of stock
Coordinated M.I.S. systems
Organized I.R.S. rulings for tax savings
Negotiated lines of credit financing
Organized building purchase, financing and additional expansion in U.S. and Europe

EDUCATION

University of Nebraska   5/72
B.S. Accounting
Certified Public Accountant License awarded   9/74

ORGANIZATIONS/ ACTIVITIES

Delegate, Republican National Convention   1988, 1992
Member, Omaha City Council   1986-88
Chair, Financial Committee, Omaha Art Museum   1987-present
Member, Omaha Chamber of Commerce   1980-present
Member, Big Brothers of Omaha   1977-present

Note: Greg has been employed by the same firm for many years. He recounts his accomplishments effectively, using very brief statements.

Ellen Epifanio

286 Lee St. #5
Teaneck, NJ 07666
(201) 520-2877

OBJECTIVE

A position in the communications industry

PERSONAL QUALIFICATIONS

Able to express concepts clearly both orally and in writing
Exceptional interpersonal and public relations skills
Conscientious, meticulous, high energy self-starter who takes great pride in work
Able to meet tight deadlines
Solid academic experience in speech and public speaking

SKILLS

RADIO AND TELEVISION PRODUCTION

Produced community-oriented television programs at MUNICIPAL CABLE STATION
Used VHS Sony and Panasonic cameras and editing equipment.
Produced scripts for upcoming programs and special projects.

Served as newscaster and promotions assistant for WNDY RADIO STATION
Developed scripts for newscasts which included leads and voiceovers.
Established clientele to promote giveaways.

Participated in all production aspects at WKML RADIO
Performed commercials.
Participated in live remotes for local companies.

PUBLIC RELATIONS AND SALES

Developed a combination of effective retail selling techniques at Towne Jewelers.
Utilized "suggestion selling" techniques, leading to effective closing and
"upselling."
Treated problem customers with patience and sensitivity, providing
restitution to ensure continued patronage.

WORK HISTORY

Student intern, City Cable Television, Hackensack, NJ, 1994
Student intern, WKML-FM Radio, Jersey City, NJ, 1994
Assistant store manager, Towne Jewelers, Montclair, NJ, 1990-1993

EDUCATION

B.A. Communication, Kean College, Union, NJ, 1994
A.A. Social Sciences, Bergen County Community College, Hackensack, NJ, 1992

*Note: Ellen is a recent college graduate whose only paid work has been in a retail store.
Notice how she features her personal qualifications and the skills she gained in her
internships. Her "objective" could be changed easily for specific jobs.*

Dennis Burdick
437 Christopher Ave. #14
Atlanta, GA 30360
404-753-9874 (voicemail)

PROFILE

Over 10 years of highly successful experience with increasing responsibility in all
   phases of the movie exhibition industry, learning from the ground up
Quick learner in converting operations from manual to automated systems
Capable of training subordinates and peers in all phases of the theater business
Excellent presentation, communication and interpersonal skills
Dedicated and motivated professional with good business acumen, able to handle
   multifaceted tasks while meeting deadlines

CAREER HISTORY

Manager, Suburban Theaters, Atlanta, GA (1993-present)
   Responsible for the entire management and operation of a multiplex theater
   including developing human resources; producing annual budget and financial
   goals; purchasing; inventory control; information processing implementation and
   maintenance; capital improvements and market development.

Raised theater evaluation from "Not-Rated" to "Gold" within a three year
   period by improving physical structure and upgrading the quality and level of
   sound and projection equipment
Implemented information processing system and troubleshot hardware
   and software
Oversaw conversion from manual to automated ticketing system
Established two new VIP accounts in each of the last 6 quarters, exceeding
   new corporate account goals
Improved concession-per-person from $1.68 to $2.07, exceeding goals by
   125% while maintaining cost goals over 3 year period
Reduced projection booth operating costs
Negotiated and managed contracts for capital projects, resulting in improved
   operational efficiencies and reduced potential liability exposure
Conducted market analysis of competition to create strategic marketing tactics
Implemented a bill scanning system, reducing the threat of receiving counterfeit money

See next page

Dennis Burdick - 2

CAREER

Assistant Manager, Suburban Theaters, Atlanta, GA
Assistant Manager, Loews Theaters, Smyrna, GA
Projectionist, United Artists Theaters, Decatur, GA
Head Usher, General Cinema, Smyrna, GA
Usher, General Cinema, Smyrna, GA

PROFESSIONAL DEVELOPMENT

Note: All of my employers have been national theater chains and all offer professional development courses. Among the more than 15 courses I have completed are:

Human Relations I & II
Management by Planning
Skills for Supervisors

Managing People
Increasing Productivity
Improving Customer Service

EDUCATION

Atlanta Technical Institute, Atlanta, GA

Stone Mountain Community College

Introduction to Computing
Troubleshooting PCs
Installing Software

Psychology 101 & 102
Introduction to Human Resources
Retailing

AFFILIATION

National Association of Theater Managers

Dennis began his career as a part-time usher in a local movie theater and now manages a multiplex. Notice how he emphasizes his accomplishments and de-emphasizes dates. The "profile" section is very well done.

TYRON EBRON
4932 Center Line Blvd.
Southfield, MI 48076
(H) 313-516-8735
(W) 313-518-4074

OBJECTIVE

A position as **Garage Supervisor** with a bus transportation company

SUMMARY

Over nine years' experience in the bus transportation industry with progressive responsibility and advancement. Have served in many operational capacities, including acting Garage Manager and Depot Master.

EXPERIENCE

Michigan Transportation Authority, Detroit, MI

Regional Supervisor, Bus Operations, Wayne County, MI
11/89-present

Master the knowledge of employees' contract and work requirements
Change schedules to reduce excessive overtime, and thus reduce costs
Handle and resolve customer complaints
Investigate accidents, vandalism and safety hazards to reduce costs of insurance and workers' compensation
Hear and resolve grievances before they go to arbitration
Assist the Garage Supervisor in hiring
Instruct over 300 new and continuing operators concerning company policy and operation

Bus Operator, Wayne County, MI   11/87-11/89

Maintained excellent on-time record on all assigned routes
Attained outstanding attendance record

Commercial Driver's License obtained 1/87

MILITARY SERVICE

Honorable Discharge, U.S. Air Force
Served in Vietnam
Member of Vietnam Veterans of America

Personal and professional references available on request.

Note: In these competitive times, more and more occupations require resumes. Here is a fine example, in a field that used to require only a handwritten job application form.

JARRETT KELLY

19 Riverview Road
Everett, MA 02149
Home (617) 883-8816
Work (617) 298-7399 ext 238
E-mail: jarrett@specialist.com

PROFILE

Over five years experience in design and development of Electro-Mechanical equipment utilizing AutoCad

Accomplished in the development of new and improved products

Capable of designing efficient and effective systems to improve productivity and reduce costs

Work well with co-workers and external customers to establish and maintain customer satisfaction

EXPERIENCE

SPECIALIST TRANSFORMERS, INC., Cambridge, MA 1993 to Present
Mechanical Engineer

Design custom enclosures for high voltage, high current AC/DC power supplies; test equipment, switches and controls

Conduct research and continual reviews of raw materials, reducing production costs

Perform extensive sheetmetal layout and PC board design

Inspect product during production and assembly, ensuring compliance to quality specifications

Travel to sites in North America, conduct surveys to determine the needs of the customer and design products to meet customer needs within cost estimations

Work and support sales to develop actual manufacturing costs to maintain profit margins

MASSACHUSETTS TRANSPORTATION AGENCY, Boston, MA 1991 to 1993
Engineering Assistant, part-time and summers

Gathered field survey data for various highway-related research projects in collaboration with project managers

Wrote reports and made presentations to management

COMPUTER EXPERIENCE

Hardware	PC Platform, MacIntosh and Mini computer environment – AS-400
Applications	AutoCad rel. 12 (use and customization), Lotus 1-2-3, Microsoft Word for Windows, Claris Works, Auto-EDMS
Operating Systems	MS-DOS, Novell Networks, Windows

EDUCATION

University of Massachusetts, Boston
Bachelor of Science Degree in Industrial Engineering
1992 (3.4 GPA)

Note: The "Profile" section skillfully weaves together skills, accomplishments, and personal qualifications. Note the use of "keywords" throughout.

Carmen Messina, M.D.

28 Sheffield Drive
Chevy Chase, MD 21090
(301) 672-0108 (Home)
(301) 788-0899 (Ans. Service)

GOAL   Partnership or staff position with HMO, multi-specialty Group Practice,
                or hospital-affiliated Group Practice

EXPERIENCE

Physician

Staff physician with Associated Medical Arts, College Park, MD   (1995-present)

Patient care in busy family medicine practice.
Treat common medical disorders including hypertension, bronchitis, asthma, diabetes.
Practice preventive medicine by screening for breast cancer, performing
        annual Pap smears, physical exams, etc.
Working in an ambulatory setting allows me to provide information and support for
        patients needing to modify their diets and lifestyles to prevent and reduce
        risks for hereditary and acquired disorders.

Emergency Room Physician

Full-time position in E.R. of Capitol Hill Hospital, Washington, DC   (1994-95)

Performed initial patient screening and diagnosis.
Handled acute emergencies including myocardial infarction, seizures,
        strokes, cardiac arrhythmia and meningitis on an emergency basis.
Triaged acute trauma victims and provided initial resuscitation and
        stabilization measures prior to transferring patients to a tertiary center.
Diagnosed and evaluated common injuries including sprains, fractures, etc.
        and provided initial treatment measures.
Diagnosed and treated common illnesses including gastroenteritis, asthma,
        pneumonia, and enteric fever.
Worked as team leader in ACLS protocol in ICU and general floors in
        addition to providing resuscitation measures in the emergency room.

PROFESSIONAL TRAINING

Residency and internship in Internal Medicine at George Washington University
Medical Center, Washington, DC (1990-94)

Third Year Resident

Worked as Team Leader on general Internal medicine floors.
Made diagnostic and therapeutic decisions about patient care and treatment.
As Senior Resident and Team Leader, responsible for running the code.
Completed Intensive Care and Coronary Care Unit rotations, including
        cardiology, ventilator management, and arterial blood gases.
Evaluated patients in Ambulatory Clinics throughout the community.

Continued on next page

Carmen Messina – 2

Second Year Resident

Supervised junior interns on general medicine floor, determining treatment plans and long-term care of hospitalized patients.

Completed rotations in Coronary Care and Intensive Care units. Worked together with Cardiologists and Pulmonologists in care of critically ill patients with septic shock, acute respiratory failure, acute renal failure, myocardial infarction, and emergency hemodialysis.

Performed invasive procedures including lumbar punctures, thoracentesis, endotracheal intubations, central venous catheters and Swan-Ganz.

First Year Resident

Treated hospitalized patients with a variety of medical conditions, including complications of diabetes, pneumonia, uncontrolled hypertension, cellulitis, exacerbation of COPD, etc.

Completed several clinical rotations, including Cardiac Step-Down Unit, General Internal Medicine, Respiratory, Neurology and Oncology.

Worked under Emergency Room doctor's supervision, with exposure to a broad range of emergency patients.

EDUCATION

Post-Doctorate Study: George Washington University, Biological Sciences (1993–94)

M.D., University of Cairo, Cairo, Egypt (1989–93)

B.S., Biological Sciences, Cairo College for Women, Cairo, Egypt (1985–89)

AWARDS

Dean's List (every semester in college and medical school), 1985–93

Class Scholar (one of 3 in medical school class), 1993

Outstanding Resident Award (voted by teaching faculty), 1994

PROFESSIONAL EXAMINATIONS

Board Certified – Internal Medicine

Foreign Medical Graduate Examination in Medical Sciences (FMGEMS), Basic Science Component – Passed 1993

Foreign Medical Graduate Examination in Medical Sciences (FMGEMS), Clinical Science Component – Passed 1994

CERTIFICATIONS

Ambulatory Care Rotation for the Community Outreach Program

Advanced Cardiac Life Support

Advanced Trauma Life Support Certificate

MEMBERSHIPS/ASSOCIATIONS

American Medical Association

American College of Physicians

Note: Carmen has been in medical practice only a short time, so she highlights her extensive training and education.

Roland Glover

c/o Samuel Glover
339 Madison Street
Florissant, MO 63031
(314) 817-2378

JOB OBJECTIVE: Emergency Medical Technician or Firefighter

CAPABILITIES

Communicate swiftly and efficiently with 911 Dispatch, Police and Fire
   authorities in emergency situations.
Exercise good judgment and leadership in crisis situations.
Capably perform all types of basic life support.
Provide excellent physical and emotional care for patients.
Maintain a clean, well-equipped ambulance, ready for any emergency.

ACCOMPLISHMENTS

Completed Squad Driving Course. Maintain an excellent personal
   driving record.
Achieved consistently high save ratios (42%) on First Aid Crew in Greene County.
Worked on first aid crew granted "most reliable status" above all crews in
   Greene County.
Awarded "Best Appearing Ambulance," Springfield Memorial Day Parade

CERTIFICATIONS & TRAINING

EMT-A, 120 Hours
CPR, American Red Cross, on-going
HAZ-MAT, Awareness Certification, 16 Hours
Heavy Vehicle Extraction, 8 Hours
Confined Space Training, 16 Hours

EXPERIENCE

EMERGENCY MEDICAL TECHNICIAN
   Davis Ambulance Service
EMERGENCY MEDICAL TECHNICIAN
   Greene County First Aid & Rescue Squad
FIREFIGHTER
   Bolivar Fire Company

EDUCATION

Graduated Walton High School, Bolivar, MO
Plan to enroll in Associate Degree Program for Fire Science,
Frontenac Community College

*Note: All of Roland's experience came as an unpaid volunteer, but he is now
applying for full-time paid positions and therefore treats volunteer work as
if it were paid work. He has created a very appealing resume.*

Walter Slepnack

229 Fetter Avenue
Sedalia, NC 27342
(910) 508-4823

PROFILE

12 years of experience in Heavy Construction industry. 10 years in utilities
construction. Present position: General Foreman

EMPLOYMENT

General Foreman, Piedmont Construction Co., Greensboro, NC (1991-present)
Responsible for the supervision of all phases of the placement and installation of
gas, electric and telephone distribution work.

> Responsible for installation of utilities using the Horizontal Directional
> Boring Method
>
> Communicate effectively the goals and objectives of each project and
> work with the assigned crew to complete work on time and within the
> established quality standards
>
> Implement knowledge of OSHA as a company Certified OSHA
> Compliance Supervisor to ensure job safety, reducing lost work
> time and insurance premiums
>
> Coach subordinates in the best methods and proper use of tools to
> improve productivity
>
> Work with company management and contractor's inspectors and
> engineers on daily basis to ensure quality of completed project
>
> Plan the most effective and efficient operations to complete projects
> and order required materials
>
> Perform repaving and landscape restoration to close out project

Heavy Construction Laborer, Piedmont Construction Co., Greensboro, NC (1987-91)
Performed as a member of a work crew all phases of gas, telephone and
electric utility work

Heavy Construction Laborer, Local 734, Greensboro, NC (1984-87)
Assigned to various heavy construction projects including road construction,
landscaping, concrete and a long-term assignment on the construction of a
sewage treatment plant

EDUCATION/TRAINING

Certification in Construction Management,
Greater Greensboro Community College, 1992

OSHA Compliance Training, 1993

Safety and Education Certification, Heavy Construction Laborer Local 734, 1991

PERSONAL

Member and elder, AME Zion Church, Sedalia, NC

*Note: Walter has progressed from laborer to a general foreman and has gone back to
school as well. His resume describes this progression nicely.*

Farid Ahmad

388 Nine Mile Rd. #6A
Highland Springs, VA 23075
(804) 611-4244

BIOLOGICAL SCIENCES/ANIMAL BEHAVIOR

SUMMARY

A recent college graduate with a solid education in biology and strong background in animal care and management.

QUALIFICATIONS

Enthusiastic, diligent worker
Excellent laboratory skills
Able to take direction well
Work effectively as a team member
Quick learner

EDUCATION

B.S., Biology, University of Virginia, June 1994
Emphasis: Zoology
GPA in major: 3.6 (on 4.0 scale)

Relevant Courses

Mammology	Microbiology	Genetics
Zoology	Organic Chemistry	Ecology
Physiology (Vertebrates)	Animal Behavior	

EMPLOYMENT

Department Manager: Mammals
Super Pet, Richmond, VA, 6/94-Present
Supervise and direct the activities of departmental staff
Interview and hire all personnel
Order all products sold in the department

Pet Groomer, Super Pet, 6/93-6/94
Full-time summer job and weekend job during school year
Responsible for grooming all animals by appointment
Groomed dogs, cats, and other mammals, including ferrets, raccoons, skunks, etc.

Veterinary Assistant, Summers, 1992, 1993
Assisted in all phases of office
Assisted in examinations and surgery

PERSONAL

Active member of biological sciences club, University of Virginia
Assistant Leader, Science Explorer Post #115
Dog handler and participant in numerous American Kennel Club sanctioned dog shows.
Handler of Grand Champion Russian Wolfhound.

Note: Here is a recent college graduate who has designed an excellent resume.
"Qualifications" and "Education" are Farid's stongest selling points.

Jane Mui-Yee, Attorney at Law
23 Pebble Creek Court
Parma, OH 44131
216-525-2911 (office) 216-284-0579 (beeper) 216-378-0104 (home)

SUMMARY OF QUALIFICATIONS

Management: Skilled in direction of research and planning in trial and pre-trial strategy
Maintain extensive client contact in high-volume practice
Accomplished negotiator and arbitrator
Supervision of large clerical staff in a law office environment

Litigation: Extensive attainments in all phases of civil litigation
Successfully conducted depositions and jury trials in personal injury cases
Vast experience in the arbitration process as a party and a mediator
Practice in all areas of Family Law including divorce, separation agreements,
adoption and child custody

CAREER HISTORY
Associate, Beauchamp & Cline, Cleveland, OH
Civil Trial Attorney
Family Law section supervisor
Extensive trial experience with busy urban law firm employing approximately
75 attorneys. (1991–present)

Associate, Cooper/Boniske, Akron, OH
Civil Trial Attorney
Supervisor of paraprofessional staff
Trial and management experience in medium-sized law firm employing
approximately 35 attorneys. (1986–91)

Law Clerk, Great Lakes Petroleum, Cleveland, OH
Review, analysis and maintenance of oil and gas leases
Assisted attorneys in drafting tax partnership agreements
Initiated conferences with landowners on behalf of company
Conducted property surveys involving oil and gas leases
Clerkship in major regional corporation that employed 10 full-time attorneys.
(1983–86)

EDUCATION
J.D., University of Akron, 1983
B.A., University of Ohio, 1978
Peace Corps Volunteer, Cambodia, 1978–80
Admitted to Ohio State Bar, 1983

*Note: This resume is quite well organized. The "Summary of Qualifications" has
two separate sections, each of interest to a prospective employer.*

Daniel Engongaro

1212 Bridge St.
Marysville, CA 95901
916-581-6436

COMPUTER SYSTEMS SUPERVISION/DATA COMMUNICATION

SUMMARY PROFILE

Offering 4 years of progressively responsible experience in computer installation and local area network management. Skilled in both technical and administrative supervision.

EXPERIENCE

United States Air Force
Edwards Air Force Base
Boron, CA
(1992-1996)

Secure Communications Systems Supervisor, Quality Assurance Inspector
Responsible for the maintenance, repair, modification and installation of all cryptographic and microcomputer systems in support of the 466th Air Base Wing. Total installation exceeded 150 computers.
Determined work procedures, estimated costs, and requisitioned needed materials. Annual budget exceeded $400,000.
Submitted justification for manpower requirements to higher headquarters and analyzed budget requirements for each fiscal year.
Assigned duties to subordinates; wrote personnel performance reports and provided counseling when needed. Supervised staff of 5.

Data Networks Team Evaluator, Team Safety Supervisor
Primary duties consisted of testing Air Force communication lines worldwide to verify conformance to government regulations using test instruments such as the Hekimian 7000 analog test set, Phoenix 500 and Firebird 5000 bit error rate test sets.
Generated reports which were forwarded to Headquarters, United States Air Force for review and action.
Responsible for an equipment account of more than $100,000.
Used protocol analyzers such as the Digilog 600 to evaluate data integrity and flow control.
Executed duties as cable fabrications expert and microcomputer repair technician for all assigned computer systems.
Special Duty Assignment requiring former Commander's endorsements and recommendations.

See page 2

Daniel Engongaro - 2

Assistant Work Center Supervisor, Squadron Safety Supervisor

Coordinated activities of up to 10 workers engaged in the installation, modification, maintenance and repair of cryptographic and teletype equipment.

Reviewed Maintenance Data Collection documentation, supply logs and trouble reports for completeness and accuracy.

Aggressively managed the work centers training program.

Key person in establishing and operating the Base Small Computer Support Center, performing duties such as base computer systems inventory, setting up computer and software training classes, performing computer maintenance and repair, and trouble shooting software problems.

Carried out base level safety duties such as building inspections and conducting spot inspections and safety meetings.

EDUCATION & TRAINING

Associates Degree in Electronic Systems Technology
Community College of the Air Force
Degree Awarded 1995

Courses included:

Narrowband Subscriber Terminal Course
Burroughs B25 E-Mail Administrator's and User's Course
Worldwide Networks Systems Evaluation Course 8
Organizational and Intermediate Maintenance
HQ AFLC Training Division "C" Language Programming Course
Logistics Systems Architects Harvard Graphics Training Program
Information Systems Technology Center Zenith Z-248 Microcomputer Repair
Communication Electronics Quality Control Procedures Course
Pacific Air Forces Quality Awareness and Unit Assessment Course
Air Mobility Command Teams and Tools Course
USAF Effective Writing Course (AFCC NCO Leadership School)
Air Force Supervisor's Course

MEMBERSHIPS

Communication Electronics Association
U.S. Air Force Reserve

PERSONAL

Willing and able to travel and/or relocate.

Note: All of Daniel's experience and education have occurred in the Air Force.
He has done an outstanding job of describing them in "civilian" language.

Rosa Chen

3842 University Ave. #42
Eugene, OR 08690
(503) 789-4657

Seeking position as a Veterinary Technician specializing in Anesthesiology.

EDUCATION

University of Oregon, Eugene, OR   B.S., Biology   October, 1994

Relevant Coursework: Applied Microbiology   Animal Physiology
                     Vertebrate Zoology   Mammalogy
                     Organic Chemistry   Genetics
                     Horse Management   Animal Behavior

Additional Studies: Graduate level Microbiology, University of Oregon, 1995

EXPERIENCE

Veterinary Technician   1992-Present
Lane Animal Hospital, Springfield, Oregon
> Assist in small animal surgery by monitoring anesthesia, heart rate and respiratory rate.
> Manage inventory of drug and food products.
> Prepare and read microscopic tests on blood, urine and feces.
> Assist in physical examination of animals.

Laboratory Assistant   1990-1992
Steek Drug Company, Eugene, Oregon   (summers)
> Prepared and conducted laboratory test of drugs being currently developed by Steek.

Voluntary Veterinary Assistant   1990-1992
Eugene Animal Shelter, Eugene, Oregon
> Assisted vets (who were also volunteers) in medical treatment of animals in the shelter.

Veterinary Assistant   1988-1990
Azalez Animal Hospital, Azalez, Oregon   (after school and summers)
> Assisted vets in all aspects of practice.

EXTRA-CURRICULAR ACTIVITIES
Programs Coordinator
Veterinary Science Club, University of Oregon - Organized field trips and speakers for VSC meetings.

INTERESTS/PERSONAL
> Fundraiser and volunteer for local small animal shelter.
> Raised $10,000 last year for shelter.
> Coordinator of area Neuter/Spay Awareness Program.

Note: Rosa is a recent college graduate with very little paid experience, but she has blended her education and unpaid experience into an outstanding resume.

JENNIFER GUPTA

27 Woodrow Street
Dorchester, MA 02124
617-831-6547 (office) 617-831-6548 (fax) 617-735-4001 (home)

SUMMARY OF QUALIFICATIONS

Experienced sales and marketing professional with a record of consistent accomplishment in pioneering and building profitable territories, exceeding planned revenue production and cost control goals, capturing and managing key accounts, developing and implementing strategic plans to penetrate uncharted markets.

Motivated self-starter with strong organizational, decision-making, communication and problem-solving skills.

SELECTED ACCOMPLISHMENTS
SALES

Pioneered new territory, increasing sales from zero to $1+ million in 1+ years.
Surpassed revenue targets by 140% of quota.
Reversed declining territory sales by reviving dormant accounts, increasing customer base and capturing new accounts.
Increased territory sales an average of 12% which contributed to substantial revenue, cash flow and profit increases.
Managed 200+ accounts concurrently, consistently growing sales and maintaining long term profitable relationships.
Forecasted and managed budgets, consistently achieving goals for revenue production and cost control.
Recruited, trained, motivated and built cohesive field sales team that consistently exceeded sales and sales-to-expense goals.

MARKETING

Directed the profitable re-launch of exclusive Salon Stylistics line, including logistics planning and timing of inventory shipments to distributors.
Coordinated planning, implementation and activities of trade shows, conventions and presentations throughout the USA.
Heightened product visibility and generated substantial new sales.
Developed highly profitable market plan, for an open product line, which was sold to salons through a multi-state distributor network.
Researched, formulated and managed programs, with focus on drug stores and beauty salons, which resulted in deep penetration of target market segments.

PROFESSIONAL EXPERIENCE

National Sales Manager, Salon Systematics, Boston MA, 1994–present
District Sales Manager, BonaVitae, Fort Lee, NJ, 1992–94
Regional Sales Manager, Biltrite Office Furniture, Philadelphia, PA, 1989–92
Sales Representative (Commercial Accounts), Freedom Furniture,
    Cherry Hill, NJ, 1988–89

Note: Jennifer put a lot of effort into this resume and it shows! Notice how succinctly she phrases her accomplishments and how well she includes "facts and figures."

CONFIDENTIAL RESUME

Wendy Hernandez

Capitol Building
Room 1440
Nashville, TN 37203
615-530-1199 office   615-530-1220 fax

Profile:

Experienced administrator who currently manages the office of the Governor of Tennessee. Especially skilled at planning and supervising complex projects.

Strengths:

Proficient in management of busy organizations with high diversity of responsibilities, needs and constituencies.

Excellent speech writer and presenter; official representative at meetings with a wide variety of groups.

Extensive marketing/public relations experience in both government and industry.

Adept at troubleshooting and problem-solving.

Skilled supervisor, able to manage both scheduling and staffing responsibilities.

Experience:

Director of Staff, Governor's Office, Nashville, TN (1992–present)
Oversee all functions of a busy office.

Supervise staff of five in scheduling travel arrangements, meetings, public forums, speeches, presentations and appearances by the Governor, his staff and the first Lady.

Represent the Governor at his meetings of municipal government representatives, mayors, special constituent groups and citizens.

Draft speeches and official correspondence for the Governor.

Marketing Director, Shapiro/Levin Attorneys at Law, Memphis, TN (1989–1992)
Developed strategic marketing plan for firm with 19 attorneys.

Organized both external and internal promotional and public relations activities for the firm.

Continued on next page

Wendy Hernandez

Represented the firm to the community at corporate, social and political events.

Composed press releases, promotional materials and presentations.

Designed presentation materials and mailings.

General Manager, Capitol City Printing, Nashville, TN (1990–92)

Supervised office and office staff for high-volume printing company with annual sales of more than $2,000,000.

Implemented new computerized office system that speeded billing and reduced costs.

Created diversified marketing plan, including newspaper, direct mail, and specialty ad placements.

Responsible for all office operations, including administration, bookkeeping, personnel and scheduling.

Additional Experience:

Executive Director, Realtors Association of Greater Memphis

Assistant Director, American Red Cross Regional Office, Memphis, TN

Office Manager, Legal Aid Society of Nashville

Assistant to the Director, Tennessee State AFL-CIO, Nashville, TN

Volunteer Experience:

Coordinator, Governor's Literacy Campaign fund-raiser

Supervised all aspects of events that raised more than $1,000,000 for literacy education.

Director, "Raise the Roof"

Oversaw entire campaign that raised more than $750,000 for Habitat for Humanity.

Assistant Coordinator, "Blood for Life"

Assisted in managing emergency blood drive that attracted more than 8,000 new donors.

Education:

Attended Tennessee State University. Major: Business Administration

PLEASE RESPECT THE CONFIDENTIALITY OF THIS RESUME

Note: Wendy has a variety of skills and has held a number of jobs. See how she describes herself first, then her paid work, and finally her volunteer work. Observe, too, how she requests confidentiality.

BRUCE A. FULLER
83 Whitney Ave.
Lincolnwood, IL 60069
(312) 892-8232 (Home)
(312) 376-4450 (Work)
(312) 828-2979 (Cellular)

OBJECTIVE

Seasoned, highly experienced management executive with extensive supervisory and personnel expertise seeks new challenges and opportunities in a firm with the potential for increased sales/profits.

EXPERIENCE

Village Market, Inc. (1985–present)

Senior Supervisor (1994–present)
Supervise 24 retail convenience stores in Northern and Western
    Chicago area with annual gross sales of $32 million.
Train managers, assistant managers and employees in all aspects
    of retail operations, including supervision, purchasing, inventory,
    scheduling, cash management, problem resolution, and profitability
    enhancement.
Participate in budget preparation for each store and monitor
    targets to ensure goals are achieved.
Inspect stores regularly to ascertain compliance with company
    policies and standards.
Coordinate with Human Resource Manager in the recruiting, hiring
    and training of store personnel and ongoing development of the
    management team.
Work closely with the Area Marketing Manager in the implementation
    of promotional programs, remodels and new stores.
Prepare extensive step-by-step training manual for store personnel.

District Supervisor (1989–94)
Directed operations of 12 stores.

Store Manager, Northern Illinois region (1986–89)
Opened 30 new locations; specialized in advancing new operations
    and establishing positive image/impact in neighborhoods.

EDUCATION

Edutech of Chicago, Schiller Park, IL
Extensive, hands-on, personalized computer training via courses
    in Windows, Project Management, Graphics, Spreadsheets
    and Database Management.

Continued on page 2

BRUCE A. FULLER
Page 2

EDUCATION
(continued)

Elmhurst College, Elmhurst, IL
National Restaurant Association Applied Food Service Sanitation
Course; earned Certification in Sanitation and Food Handling.

Belmont University, Chicago, IL
Food Management and Marketing

Dale Carnegie, Chicago, IL
Effective Speaking & Human Relations

ORGANIZATIONS

Member, Greater Chicago Chamber of Commerce
Member, Illinois Food Council
Member, Greater Chicago Food Council

CHARITABLE ACTIVITIES

Arden Institute for Autism

Advisory Panel for employment of the handicapped.
10–year fundraising and organizational volunteer.
Raised in excess of $500,000 for the Institute.
Assisted in fundraising for construction of Village House for
        diagnosis and treatment of autism in infants and children to age 5.
Established Village Care Mobile Unit to bring diagnostic and
        treatment services for autism to the community.
Helped initiate Village Camp for autistic children and families.

Children's Miracle Network
        Aid in special events and fundraising for nationwide network assisting
        children and their families with serious illnesses.

Mission House
        Assist in organization of annual Christmas party for over
        1,200 Mission House children at the MacCormick Convention Center.

Note: Here is an excellent way to handle experience with only one employer.
The "Charitable Activities" demonstrate strong commitment to the community.

EMMA SCHLESINGER
22 Westmoreland Road
Remerton, GA 31602
(912) 985-0423

CAREER OBJECTIVE: Seeking a position in Banking, Credit, or Customer Service.

STRENGTHS: Over ten years of experience in finance and banking-related fields.

EXPERIENCE:
Cashier, Valdosta State College, Valdosta, GA
  Cash personal checks, credit union checks, process petty cash vouchers and expense reports
  Organize and distribute bi-monthly payrolls
  Order and maintain cash balance
  Sell travelers checks, accept payments for miscellaneous accounts and refunds to company
  Summarize and account for all financial activity

Head Teller/Assistant Operations Manager
First National Bank of Georgia, Valdosta, GA
  Supervise and evaluate bank tellers
  Order and ship cash; maintain cash level in branch
  Oversee audits and safe deposits
  Buy and sell foreign currency; prepare international drafts
  Extensive customer service; MAC machine settlement

Senior Client Services Representative
Lowndes County Medical Center, Valdosta, GA
  Oversee financial services for patients and staff
  Telephone and written correspondence with physicians and other medical providers
  Monthly summary and analysis of Credit Union activities
  Assist internal as well as external auditors
  Special accounting projects as assigned by manager

Teller and Platform Assistant, First Bank of Lowndes, Valdosta, Ga
  Teller functions
  Open savings and checking accounts
  Interview potential loan candidates

EDUCATION:
B.S., Business Administration
Valdosta State College, Anticipated 1996

REFERENCES: Available upon request

Note: Emma is an adult learner presently enrolled in college. Although she has not had high-level jobs, she articulates her responsibilities well.

CHRISTOPHER CROUX
331 Middleton Rd.
Lewiston, ME 04240
(207) 622-1974

BACKGROUND
22 years in the construction business, from framer to carpenter to general contractor.

Proficient in all aspects of construction from laying out footings with transit to the finish trim
Experienced foreman and crew chief
Skilled cabinet and woodworking craftsman
Qualified in all types of custom laminating work

EXPERIENCE
CHRIS CROUX CONSTRUCTION COMPANY, Lewiston, ME (1982 - present)

Owner of General Contracting business. Maintain an average work force of five employees.
Handle a variety of jobs including:
   Complete renovation of 14-unit apartment building
   Renovation of retail furniture store
   Remodeling of French theme restaurant
   Remodeling and renovation of residential properties including patios, additions,
      dormers, cabinets and built-in wall units
   Specialize in building custom homes
   Built 8 homes in first 10 years in my own business

BILL BREWER CONTRACTING, Portsmouth, NH (1976- 1982)

Worked as Foreman and Lead Carpenter for a general contractor specializing in commercial
and industrial construction. Examples of completed jobs are:
   A 40,000 square foot annex to a hospital building
   Total renovation of the main post office in Portsmouth
   New classroom wing of local middle school

EDUCATION
Coastal Community College
Two years of night courses in Drafting, Design, and Blueprints

REFERENCES
Extensive references available from a wide range of clients

Note: The "background" is actually a "Qualifications Summary." Excellent use of specific examples throughout resume.

STEPHANIE CHERNOFF

322 1/2 Easton Ave.
West Bridgewater, GA 02379
(912) 474-3082

CAREER GOAL To secure a managerial position in sales or marketing.

CAREER SUMMARY   10 years of sales, marketing and supervisory experience, with a focus on printed and packaging materials. Skills in building direct and distributor business growth.

STRENGTHS
Outstanding track record in sales and marketing
Highly motivated and goal-oriented
Excellent communication skills
Skilled sales closer

EXPERIENCE
Sales Manager, Prime Packaging, Brockton, MA (1992-1995)
Developed $4 million in new business.
Initiated a line of custom boxes that generated more than $1 million in sales
Managed a sales force of 10 representatives, in plant and on the road
Manufacturers of corrugated based promotional packaging, printed index tab dividers and custom file folders.

Sales Representative, Tab Products, Providence, RI (1990-1992)
One of the top 3 sales representatives nationally in percentage over quota:
four consecutive years
Over four years increased business from $485,000 per year to over
$2 million per year (corporate average less than 10 percent per year growth)
Coordinated a telemarketing program that was so successful that it was
adopted nationally
Sales of Printed Index Tab Dividers: retail, wholesale, printing trade

Key Account Manager, Pawtucket Paper Products, Pawtucket, RI (1987-1989)
Increased sales from $19,000 monthly to $58,000 monthly in two years
Responsibilities included establishing new accounts and servicing existing accounts
Paper Wholesaler selling to commercial printers

EDUCATION
Bachelor of Science Degree, Management
University of Connecticut, Storrs, CT 1987

Note: The section headed "Strengths" will certainly get an employer's attention. Stephanie describes each employer after she details her accomplishments.

ALBERT KAHN
607 Sayre Ave.
Hoboken, NJ 07030
(201) 715-2280

SUMMARY
Experienced Director of Hotel Security seeks position in Western U.S.

EXPERIENCE
The Algonquin, New York, NY
Director of Security 6/91-Present
 Develop security-related policies and procedures that have enhanced the
 hotel operation
 Coordinate the security arrangements for visiting dignitaries,
 entertainers and executives of Fortune 500 Companies
 Responsible for Security and Fire Safety training of more than 200 hotel
 employees
 Supervise staff of 15

The Ritz-Carlton, Boston, MA
Director of Security 2/86-6/91
 Instituted, as well as restructured, security and safety policies for this
 exclusive 4-star hotel
 Coordinator and liaison with government agencies for the security of
 visiting international Heads of State and dignitaries
 Supervised security measures for CEOs of Fortune 500 companies
 Supervised and managed a department of 12 Security Officers and Time
 keepers

The Helmsley Park, New York, NY
 Assistant Director of Security 10/84-2/86
 Hotel Assistant Manager 6/83-10/84
 Security Officer 1/82-6/83

EDUCATION
City University of New York, New York, NY
Bachelor of Science Degree, Criminal Justice

REFERENCES
Available upon request.

Please respect the confidentiality of this resume.

*Note: Albert relies on his most recent jobs, both at well-known hotels, to secure
interviews in a new geographical region.*

DIANA KHOURY

Dental Hygienist
3312 Westpoint Way
Stock Island, FL 33040
(305) 294-3302

QUALIFICATIONS

Skilled dental hygienist. Good rapport with dentists and patients. Specialty in periodontics. Expertise in all areas of general practice dentistry. Knowledgeable in office procedures. Devoted to patient education.

EXPERIENCE

Dental Hygienist, Roberta Alomar, D.D.S., Periodontist, Key West, FL (1992–Present)

    Perform oral prophylaxis.
    Place and remove periodontal dressings.
    Take and develop x-rays.
    Record patient histories.

    Note: Dr. Alomar is relocating her practice to Colorado in the spring of 1997

Dental Hygienist, Emily Jenkins, D.D.S., General Dentistry, Columbia, SC (1990–1992)

    Performed all dental hygienist functions in busy office.

Office Assistant, Wendall Franklin, D.D.S., General Dentistry, Chapel Hill, NC (1988–1990)

    Part-time position in front office of solo practitioner. Learned administrative functions of office, including scheduling, billing, insurance, etc.

EDUCATION

    College of Medicine & Dentistry
    University of North Carolina, Chapel Hill, NC
        Periodontal Certification 1990
        Dental Hygiene Certification 1988
    Appalachian State University, Boone, NC, Attended 1985–1987

PERSONAL

    Volunteer hygienist at Cayo Hueso Free Clinic, Key West

Note: The "Qualifications" section is an outstanding feature of this resume.
Diana includes her reason for leaving her present job.

Helen Kashimura

81347 Venice Blvd., Apt.102
Culver City, CA 90230
(213) 794-3420

OBJECTIVE

Conscientious, detail-oriented recent graduate seeking position as Paralegal

EDUCATION

A.A.S., Legal Studies, Santa Monica City College, December 1995

Dean's List; GPA 3.5

Extensive computer experience with WordPerfect 5.1 and Lotus 1-2-3

Relevant coursework includes:

Domestic Relations	Civil Litigation
Survey of Torts	Business Law 1 & 11
Legal Research & Writing	Wills & Probate
Real Estate Transactions	Corps. & Partnerships

EXPERIENCE

Intern, WomanCenter, Santa Monica, CA 9/95-12/95
    Counseled abused women on their legal rights and prerogatives.
    Accompanied clients to court.
    Interacted with judges on selected cases.

City of Los Angeles Police Department 11/89 - 11/94
Technical Assistant, Health Benefits Section
    Counseled active employees on their health benefits and plan options.
    Developed expertise in language and details of forms for various
        health plans.
    Extensive telephone contact and computer operations.
    Skilled in dictation and word processing.
    Promoted to Technical Assistant from Senior Clerk.

INTERESTS

Competitive rider and trainer in dressage. Have won three ribbons in
regional (Western States) competition.

REFERENCES

Available on request.

Note: Willing to travel or relocate

*Note: Helen went back to school while she was employed. Like any recent graduate
she emphasizes her relevant coursework and treats her internship like a job.*

WILLIAM NEWKIRK
87342 Mokauea Ave., Apt 44
Honolulu, HI 96816
(808) 871-1762

OBJECTIVE
Naval Flight Officer seeks civilian position in organization that requires skills in management and supervision—and values capable, level-headed leadership.

MILITARY EXPERIENCE / UNITED STATES NAVY
Lieutenant, Assistant Air Department Officer
Naval Air Warfare Center, Honolulu, HI (January 1990 - December 1995)

Responsible for air operations, aviation support equipment maintenance, computer security and staff training. Supervised 25 air traffic controllers, 15 equipment maintenance technicians, and 10 aircraft line handlers.
   Reduced staffing by 35% with no loss in operational capability
   Reduced cost of aircraft maintenance by 25%
   Oversaw transition to new computer system

Ensign, Lieutenant Junior Grade
Naval Air Preparedness Center, Norfolk, VA (March 1987 - December 1989)

Navigator/Communicator and tactical coordinator.
Selected as Squadron Readiness Officer by superiors.
   Shaped 130 personnel into 11 fully capable aircrews ready for deployment
   Had sole responsibility for qualifying, training and scheduling all 11 crews

Naval Flight Officer Training
San Diego, CA; Brunswick, ME; Pensacola, FL (August 1986 - February 1987)

Successfully completed prestigious 18-month training program, which included more than 50 sorties in actual flight as well as simulations in 6 different Navy and Air Force aircraft.

EDUCATION
   B.S., Aeronautics & Aeronautical Engineering, 1986
   University of South Carolina, Charleston, S.C.
      Naval ROTC scholarship for last 3 years of college
      Phi Eta Sigma national scholastic honor society, elected member
      Top 10% of Naval ROTC class
      Sigma Chi fraternity, Chapter President 1985-86

Note: Excellent use of "facts and figures" throughout resume. Good example of how to treat military experience as work experience.

David Ng
2936 White Pine Road
Ammon, ID 83406
(208) 987-2863

CAREER SUMMARY

Skilled salesperson with extensive experience in freight shipping. Strong record in acquiring and servicing new accounts. Outstanding customer relations skills.

EMPLOYMENT HISTORY

Account Manager, InterMountain Freight, Idaho Falls, ID (1994–present)
- Increased sales over 57% from 1993 to 1995
- Manage 175 to 200 accounts
- Give sales presentations to and interact with present and prospective customers
- Consistently one of top performers in region

Account Manager, Western Transport, Pocatello, ID (1992–1993)
- Managed 200 to 250 accounts in five states
- Strong in customer interaction, dealing well with clients on a one-to-one basis
- Resolved claims and service problems
- Acquired at least 50 new accounts

Note: Western Transport closed Pocatello terminal in November 1991

Outbound Supervisor, Domino Trucking, Las Vegas, NV (1991–1992)
- Supervised dock crew to properly load road trailers
- Kept track of dock production of each crew member
- Held conferences with workers who needed training or discipline
- Held safety meetings with all workers

Inbound Supervisor, Domino Trucking, Las Vegas, NV (1989–1991)
- Supervised dock crew to properly unload road trailers
- Maintained proper level of discipline and order on dock at all times

Note: This position was part-time while I completed college

EDUCATION

B.S., Physical Education
University of Nevada – Las Vegas

PERSONAL Speak conversational Spanish. Regularly use computers on the job.

Note: David has captured the key responsibilities of each job in his short, clear statements. The resume layout focuses attention on responsibilities.

MUKTEESHWAR GANDE
88 Columbia Street
Lawrence, KS 66025
(913) 379-2009 Home
(913) 985-3493 Office

POSITION DESIRED: BOOK PRODUCTION DIRECTOR

SKILLS & QUALIFICATIONS
Recognized as an effective negotiator and decision maker
Rewarded for consistently reducing production costs by 20-40%
Thoroughly knowledgeable about book publishing and manufacturing techniques
Experienced with all aspects of trade, college, reference, and art books
Able to manage complex projects from initial design concept through final
  production
Persistent, thorough, and prompt in completing projects, meeting deadlines,
  and staying within estimated costs
Enthusiastic, energetic worker, excellent in a team setting
Capable supervisor with strong people skills

WORK EXPERIENCE
Production Manager
University Press of Kansas, Lawrence, KS 1991 - present
Responsible for the entire production process for art and archaeology books,
  as well as other heavily illustrated books: approximately 20 titles per year
Negotiate contracts and bids with overseas and U.S. suppliers, constantly
  evaluating their performance
Prepare production budgets for every book
Administer effective quality control, cost containment and scheduling in the
  management of complex museum quality art books
Effectively negotiate purchases, often resulting in $5,000 - $25,000 in savings
Develop liaisons with manufacturers, in-house personnel, editors, sales,
  marketing, and free-lance designers

Production Manager, W.W. Norton, New York, NY 1984 - 1991
Reprint Manager, Basic Books, New York, NY 1982 - 1984

EDUCATION
M.A., English Literature, University of Calcutta
Certificate, Book Production, University of Pennsylvania

U.S. Citizen since 1981

*Note: Terrific use of skills and qualifications, nicely blended together.
Wise note about citizenship.*

SUSAN LIEBERMAN
17 Terril Way
Ypsilanti, MI 48197 · (517) 748-0321

OBJECTIVE: A position leading to a career in finance

EDUCATION

M.B.A., Finance, University of Michigan, Expected June 1997
B.S., With highest honors, University of Minnesota, June 1992

PERSONAL PROFILE

Exposure to various aspects of business, including finance, accounting, human resources, marketing and merchandising. Special talent for using innovative and resourceful methods in problem solving, time management and planning. Adaptable, able to learn quickly.

PROFESSIONAL SKILLS

Management: Interviewed, hired and trained staff. Responsible for all aspects of operating retail store.
Analysis: Monitored inventory stock levels, selling and merchandise trends to make purchasing decisions and optimize business profits.
Budgeting: Analyzed monthly department spending as related to targeted budget. Created spreadsheets to organize data and compute information for presentation.
Marketing: Coordinated monthly fashion shows and promotions which generated business and improved customer relations.
Communication: Excellent selling techniques and ability to communicate with people, as well as outstanding writing skills.
Computer: Proficient in Lotus, WordPerfect, and FoxPro. Provided spreadsheet support for various departments in Technical Operations.

PROFESSIONAL ACHIEVEMENTS

Enhanced Training: Developed a training program to enhance employee product knowledge and selling skills which was adopted by stores throughout the company. Placed 60% of my store staff into managerial positions.
Increased Productivity: Created store contests and meetings to motivate staff and maintain standards of customer service, resulting in a 30% increase in annual sales.
Improved Customer Service: Awarded "Outstanding Retailer" by Main Place Mall for excellence in customer service. Received annual Productivity Award from corporate office.

EMPLOYMENT HISTORY

Senior Assistant to Director of Human Resources, W.K. Kellogg, BattleCreek, MI
        (July 1994 - Present)
Manager, Jeans Plus, Main Place Mall, St. Paul, MN (December 1992 - June 1994)
        Began as clerk while in college and progressed to Assistant Manager upon
        graduation. Appointed manager within six months.

Note: Susan put a lot of effort into identifying and grouping her skills and achievements. She has included "keywords" throughout.

MODESTO LITTLEDOVE

36812 Salinas Drive
Casa Grande, Arizona 85226
(602) 292-1714

OBJECTIVE

Seeking day-shift position in nursing

EXPERIENCE

Staff Nurse, Medical/Surgical Floor
Desert Center Hospital, Maricopa, Arizona

Staff Nurse, Oncology
Desert Center Hospital, Maricopa, Arizona

Licensed Practical Nurse
Hot Springs Nursing Home, Hot Springs, Arizona

EDUCATION

Enrolled in R.N. Certificate Program
Maricopa Community College

Associate's Degree in Nursing
Maricopa Community College

Licensed Practical Nurse Certification
Hot Springs Area Education Center

PERSONAL

President, Parent-Teacher Association, Hernando Soto Elementary School
Volunteer, American Cancer Society, Southern Chapter
Assistant Scoutmaster, Girl Scout Troop #153

REFERENCES

Angelina Hernandez, Nursing Supervisor, Hot Springs Nursing Home (602) 791-1812

Evelyn Katonah, M.D., Director, On-Call Emergency Care Center (602) 864-8227

Fay Ohnuki, Principal, Hernando Soto Elementary School (602) 793-2318

Note: Here is a working mother, who has worked both full and part-time and gone back to school. Dates would only be confusing. She works in a field that requires references.

JULIUS CARR

911 Cedar Lane #4
Superiour, MN 55807
(218) 903-0421

CAREER SUMMARY

More than 10 years of experience designing and implementing user friendly software applications for laboratory process control, data acquisition, data analysis and data display on large scale projects. Work with extreme accuracy under pressure:

HARDWARE EXPERIENCE:	VAX Family, SUN Workstations, Gould
OPERATING SYSTEMS:	VMS, UNIX, MPX
LANGUAGES:	FORTRAN, C, IDL
SOFTWARE:	INGRES, SQL

WORK EXPERIENCE

Applications Software Engineer, Physical Systems, Inc., Duluth, MN 1987 - present
Responsible for the design, implementation and maintenance of software applications using real-time control, data acquisition, data analysis and graphics for major physics projects measuring extreme densities and temperatures.

Interfaced with end-user physicists, hardware engineers and systems programmers from
initial requirements, design and implementation through maintenance and enhancements
Served as Engineer-in-Charge to field questions and problems of physicists during experiments.
Diagnosed and solved hardware and software problems
Provided orientation and support to contract programmers

Programmer/Analyst, Southwest Oil Services, Durango, CO 1982 - 1987
Primary duties involved the design and implementation of software used in oil exploration.

Designed and implemented database and graphics programs used by management and
scientists as their major software tool
Designed and implemented process control software of automated test systems measuring
spectral responses of photomultiplier tubes under computer controlled conditions

EDUCATION

Bachelor of Science, University of Arizona, Tucson, AZ 1981
Major: Computer Science   Minor: Earth and Environmental Sciences

PERSONAL

Worked my way around the world on oil tankers after graduating from college
Volunteer computer teacher in school district's "Professionals in the Classroom" program

*Note: The use of technical jargon is to be expected from a software designer.
The "jargon" contains numerous "keywords."*

Jason Harris
812 Jefferson St.
New Haven, IN 46774
(812) 605-3423

OBJECTIVE
Fitness counselor in a corporate facility where experience in the health field and human sciences will be utilized by an employer to enhance and contribute to corporate goals.

PERSONAL PROFILE
Experienced in fitness environment; skilled in customizing general programs and equipment to meet the needs of individuals. Self-directed with proven leadership and decision-making skills, as well as ability to learn fast and follow directions. People skills with strong ability in written and oral communication as well as one-on-one and group instruction. Organized and detail-oriented.

PROFESSIONAL SKILLS
Instruction: Created and instructed an aerobic interval training class which encompassed five pieces of fitness apparatus to improve cardiovascular fitness.

Diagnostic Testing: Interacted with cardiac diagnostic team of major medical center. Experience included exposure to stress testing, echocardiographic analysis, and exercise prescription.

Communication: Lectured corporate staff in wellness-oriented subjects such as lower back care, nutrition and hypertension.

Management: Supervised daily activities of Fitness Center including maintenance of equipment, administrative tasks, and interfacing with office and medical staff.

Organization: Involved in establishment of NCR Fitness Center, which entailed designing promotional material, field testing, supervising and evaluating performance of participants.

Planning: Coordinated various activities such as ticket sales, correspondence, paperwork and training of crew members necessary in the implementation of a major promotional event. 40,000 people attended.

EDUCATION
B.S., Corporate Fitness, Wayne State University, September, 1989 to May 1994.
Related courses: Anatomy & Physiology I & 11, Exercise Physiology, Kinesiology, Nutrition, General Biology I & II, and Fitness in Business & Industry.

EMPLOYMENT HISTORY
Fitness Center Supervisor   NCR Corporation
May 1992 to August 1992   Manufacturing Firm

Fitness Assistant   Pro Fitness
Internship - May 1991 to August 1991   Corporate Fitness Consulting Firm

Cardiac Rehabilitation Assistant   St. Thomas Medical Center
Internship - May 1990 to August 1991   Cardiac Rehabilitation Unit

Note: "Personal Profile" mixes skills and qualifications, while "Professional Skills" includes accomplishments. Boldface type is very effective.

PAULA RAMSEY, A.C.S.W.
Clinical Social Worker
347 Stillwater Way
Middletown, KY 40223
Office: (502) 834-4646
Answering Service: (502) 247-3007

CERTIFICATIONS   Certified Board Diplomate in Clinical Social Work, 1991
N.A.S.W. Diplomate in Clinical Social Work, 1989
A.C.S.W., 1985

EDUCATION   M.S.W., Social Casework Concentration
University of Kentucky, Louisville, KY 1983
B.A., Sociology, Berea College, Berea, KY, 1981

EXPERIENCE
Director of Clinical Services
CATHOLIC FAMILY SERVICES
Louisville, KY 1992 - present

Oversee all clinical programs including personal counseling, suicide prevention, family abuse mediation, community outreach, and substance abuse treatment.

Supervise staff of 8 full-time and 4 part-time M.S.W. social workers
Supervise 5 support staff and paraprofessionals
Supervise 4-6 graduate student interns

Clinical Director
THE CRISIS CENTER
Louisville, KY 1989 - 1992
Supervised all-volunteer staff at 24-hour crisis "hotline"
Responsible for training and scheduling staff of more than 80 hotline counselors

Previous experience includes social work positions with public and private agencies in several cities within Kentucky

PERSONAL
Placed 3rd in 1994 10-mile "Fun Run" sponsored by Louisville Charities Council
Volunteer coach of the "Hurricanes" pee-wee soccer team

Note: In a field where certifications and education are significant, Paula lists these first. She focuses on her most recent experience and assumes that she will discuss her first eight years of work when she interviews.

ANGELA J. GARCIA

2684 Fountain Lane
Lafayette, CO 80026
(303) 808-9425

OBJECTIVE

Seeking challenging position in the field of Drug and Alcohol Counseling, Testing, Interviewing, or Research

EDUCATION

B.A., Psychology, May 1995   University of Colorado, Boulder, CO

EXPERIENCE

VOLUNTEER, PROJECT HELP, BOULDER, CO
Intake worker for people living with AIDS.

Includes interviewing to assess risk taking behavior, personal stability, apparent level of distress and service needs. Provide crisis counseling and crisis intervention on an as-needed basis and assist in obtaining entitlements, health care, housing and other services.

INTERN, BOULDER HOUSE, BOULDER, CO
Counselor at general psychiatric/alcohol and drug abuse treatment facility.
Worked in Dual Diagnosis program under direction of Psychiatric Social Worker:

Facilitated adjunctive therapy groups.
Conducted some one-to-one counseling sessions.
Participated in daily Dual Diagnosis Meetings.
Attended daily General Staff Meetings.
Completed billing and patient charting.
Helped set up aftercare.
Followed-up on aftercare arrangements after discharge.

INDEPENDENT STUDY

DIABETES CLINIC, BOULDER MEDICAL CENTER, BOULDER, CO.

Researched coping skills of adolescents with insulin-dependent diabetic mellitus and their parents. Observed patients' and families' behavior.

ROCKY MOUNTAIN PSYCHIATRIC HOSPITAL, BOULDER, CO.

Facility treating Mentally Ill/Chemically Addictive (MICA) patients. Designed and developed interview forms for research project on treatment plans for dual diagnosis patients. Interviewed patients and staff about dual treatment plan.

Note: Here is an entire resume without paid work experience. Notice how Angela has treated her unpaid experience just as if it were a "real" job.

Margaret Crosby-Lewis

84 Creek Road
Bonner, MT 59823
(406) 862-2062

GOAL

Seeking part-time position as medical assistant. Special expertise in management of diabetes.
Excellent interpersonal skills.

EDUCATIONAL QUALIFICATIONS

Western Montana Community College
Medical Assistant Training Program
Graduated 1995
Montana State University
B.S., Biology, 1980

Most recent training included:

ADMINISTRATIVE
scheduling
medical records management
medical transcription
accounting/billing
patient relations

CLINICAL
medical histories
laboratory procedures
taking vital signs
sterilizing instruments
patient education

Certified Medical Assistant
Member, American Association of Medical Assistants

BACKGROUND

American Diabetes Association
President, Diabetes Association of Missoula (local chapter)
Served two terms: 1986-1988; 1990-1992
Delegate to state association from Missoula chapter, 1989-1990

Have lectured throughout western part of state on diabetes and insulin management
Have attended numerous workshops on diabetes

PERSONAL

Single parent of teenage diabetic child. Able to work up to 30 hours per week.

Note: Margaret has completed a training program after 15 years of working in the home and as a volunteer. Her son was severely diabetic when he was younger. Her resume makes the most of her recent training and her volunteer work.

GAIL GALLOWAY

27843 Canyon Dr, Apt 22
Mesa, AZ 85016
(602) 493-1337

QUALIFICATIONS

Experienced sportswear and accessories buyer who has consistently exceeded sales goals. Knowledgeable in all aspects of retail clothing store operations and purchasing.

EXPERIENCE

Buyer, Sportswear

FASHIONS WEST, Phoenix, AZ (Corporate Headquarters) 1994 - present

Function:

Responsible for all aspects of buying and merchandising sportswear for chain of 15 stores with annual sales volume over $4 million

Accomplishments:

Generated a 25% increase in sportswear sales in two years

Increased sportswear sales from 70-80% of total company's sales volume in two years

Worked closely with manufacturers to develop exclusive merchandise for stores

Planned, purchased for and attended new store openings

Developed sportswear sales plans for all 15 stores

Manager

CAREER CORNER, Tucson, AZ 1991 - 1994

Function:

Managed a $2 million retail clothing store

Accomplishments:

Hired, trained and developed staff of eight

Increased sales by more than 10% per year

Maintained high level of communication with own staff members and upper management to ensure company objectives were met

Assistant Buyer

I.MAGNIN, Los Angeles, CA 1989 - 1991

Function:

Active partner in coordinating procurement, store distribution and seasonal sales/stock plans

Accomplishments:

Purchased more than $10 million per year in sportswear and accessories

Projected seasonal advertising plans by determining advertisement strategies in each geographic market and determined productivity of advertisements through analysis of computerized retail buying records

EDUCATION

SYRACUSE UNIVERSITY
Bachelor of Science Degree
Retailing & Marketing   Grade point average in major: 3.6 (on 4.0 scale)

Note: Gail outlines her functions and accomplishments for her most recent jobs in a very appealing way.

Kristen Caruso

87 Woodland Drive
Wyoming, DE 19901
(302) 868-5277

OBJECTIVE

A product development position which will utilize my technical design skills
in electrical engineering.

WORK EXPERIENCE

Product Development Engineer
Fluortech, Inc. January, 1994 - Present
Work to develop state-of-the-art fluorescent lamp ballasts for small start-up
company. Develop products from the conceptual stage to the production level.

Responsible for:
- Circuit design and documentation
- Component specification and sourcing
- PCB Design
- UL listing procedures and quality procedures
- Resolving quality issues
- Managing six-terminal LAN system

TECHNICAL EXPERIENCE

CAD for schematics, PCB layout and auto-routing, AutoCAD
LANtastic Network OS and related hardware
Pascal, BASIC, Assembly languages for TMS320C25, 8088,
8051, PSPICE and Microcap simulation programs

EDUCATION

University of Delaware
Bachelor of Science, January, 1994
Major: Electrical Engineering

Designed Voice Recognition System using TMS320 DSP chip.
Researched speech theory and recognition algorithms for use in
assembly program. (Senior Project, January - December, 1993)

*Note: Kristen has had only one job, but she has clearly spelled out her
responsibilities. The "Technical Experience" section is also a "keyword summary."*

MARCUS BARTRAM
12 Gorman Rd.
Pittsfield, MA 01201
(413) 903-3423 Office
(413) 903-5324 Ans. Service

CAREER SUMMARY

Over 15 years experience maintaining and repairing Air Conditioning, Refrigeration and Commercial Electrical Products. My experience, combined with knowledge gained from running my own business, can contribute to any maintenance program or organization.

EMPLOYMENT HISTORY

Owner/Operator, BOYTON SERVICE COMPANY, Somerville, MA   (10/91-Present)

Responsible for the day to day operations of a successful commercial and residential air conditioning, heating and electrical repair and installation company.

   Manage three employees
   Ensure company profitability
   Oversee sub-contractors (up to 15 per year)
   Purchase, install and repair commercial kitchens for hospitals and restaurants
   Repair and sell used electrical equipment with quality service

Manager, Maintenance and Repairs, FRIENDLY'S ICE CREAM PARLORS   (10/88-10/91)

Sole individual responsible for maintaining refrigeration, air-conditioning, electrical equipment, plumbing and heating for 10 Friendly's franchises throughout region.

   Hired sub-contractors
   Purchased equipment and parts amounting to $40,000 to $50,000 per year
   Oversaw sub-contractors during the building of new locations and repair of existing locations

HVAC "A" Mechanic, DIGITAL EQUIPMENT CORPORATION   (2/86-10/88)

Responsibilities involved the maintenance and repair of various chillers, compressors, motor control stations, hot water and steam heating systems, exhaust hoods for laboratory use, cooling water towers, pumping systems (electric and steam turbine).

   Maintained and repaired 10 Edpack computer room coolers and 19 microprocessor controlled constant temperature chambers

SEE NEXT PAGE

MARCUS BARTRAM EMPLOYMENT HISTORY (continued)

Diagnosed electronic, electric and pneumatic control systems, air balance and calibration of VAV equipment, Powers 600 computer system and boiler maintenance
Supervised up to six workers when required

HVAC Mechanic, BOSTON MEDICAL CENTER   (4/84-2/86)

Responsibilities included the maintenance, repair and installation of various chillers, pneumatic equipment and controls, air compressors, vacuum pumps, commercial refrigeration, heating systems, water tower, water pumps and a domestic hot water system

Performed arc and gas welding, brazing, blueprint reading and pipefitting
Troubleshot wiring problems and various related maintenance jobs

HVAC Installer, YANKEE MANUFACTURING COMPANY   (8/83-4/84)

Responsibilities included installation of heaters (gas and oil), air cleaners, air conditioners, full conversions, duct-work, and thermostats.

Made custom duct-work
Bought various equipment for installation
Performed all aspects of sheet metal fabrication

EDUCATION

MASSACHUSETTS TECHNICAL INSTITUTE, Boston, MA
September 1983-January 1984
Air Conditioning and Refrigeration

CAMBRIDGE COMMUNITY COLLEGE, Boston, MA
January 1984-Present
Air Conditioning and Refrigeration (Electrical Controls, Electronics)

SPECIAL COURSES/SEMINARS ATTENDED

Bitzer Steam Heating Seminar; Trane Centrifugal Seminar;
Chemtrol PVC Pipefitting Seminar; Black Seal Preparation Course;
Betz Chemicals Steam Boiler Seminar; Welding Course;
Honeywell Pneumatic Control Set-up and Maintenance Seminar

AWARDS

Certificate of Merit, Massachusetts Technical Institute, January 1984

Note: Marcus promotes his experience by presenting his responsibilities and then highlighting key features. His resume demands a second page.

WILLIAM KRASNANSKY
832 Estates Blvd., Apt. 1
Needmore, IN 46516
(812) 870-9334 (car)
(812) 853-5790 (home)

QUALIFICATIONS

Sales professional, with accomplishments in sales and sales management in commercial accounts and retail establishments selling varied products.

Experienced in all phases of the sales process, including prospecting, closing sales, customer and credit follow-up.

Able to quickly apply sales experience to new products.

A "self-starter" and tireless worker who produces results.

EXPERIENCE

Area Manager, Commercial Division, Alta Fuels Co., Elkhart, IN   (1992 to present)

Total responsibility for developing a new commercial division of independent fuel company. Responsibilities included generating prospects, selling, credit and customer service of newly originated commercial accounts.

Established new commercial sales division

Increased sales from zero gallons to 2.5 million gallons in six months

Area Manager, Enviro, Inc., Kokomo, IN   (1987-1992)
Responsible for geographic area within commercial division of fuel company. Responsibilities included prospecting, placing orders, credit and customer service of commercial accounts.

Built business unit from zero gallons to 6 million gallons in sales of fuel products to large commercial accounts such as UPS, Upland Dairy, and others

Developed new sales regions in Kokomo and Elkhart

Called on all levels of management, including VP's, General Managers, Purchasing Managers, and others

CONTINUED ON NEXT PAGE

WILLIAM KRASNANSKY
Page 2

Sales Representative, A-I Chemical Products, Gary, IN   (1985-1987)

   Responsible for calling on new and existing accounts to place janitorial
   cleaning supplies, chemicals and paper products. Handled all phases of
   sales process.

   Exceeded sales goals on a regular basis

   Signed up more than 50 new accounts in 3 years

Route Driver/Sales Representative, Uniform Cleaning Services, Grand Rapids, MI
                                                                          (1982-1985)

   Responsible for calling on new and existing accounts to secure uniform
   cleaning services

   Received performance bonus each year

   Added more than 10 new, large-volume customers each year

Retail Store Manager, Kinney Shoes, Grand Rapids, MI   (1983-1985)

   Total responsibility for all operations of retail shoe store.Responsibilities included
   all personnel functions, training, merchandising, budgets and expenses.

   Managed from 8 - 12 employees in several different stores

   Increased annual sales to more than $3 million in each store

PERSONAL

Can speak conversational French and some Italian

Volunteer fundraiser for Muscular Dystrophy Foundation for more than 10
years. Have personally raised over $1 million.

Volunteer assistant in pediatric physical therapy department of St. Xavier
Hospital, Elkhart, TN

*Note: Salespeople need to demonstrate their sales accomplishments. Bill does this
job by job. He never attended college, so he doesn't have a section for education.
He uses the "Personal " heading to show that he has a life beyond work.*

ROY HOROWITZ
4-8 Porthault Street
Three Rivers, MI 49093
(616) 993-2087

OCCUPATIONAL OBJECTIVE

Experienced journeyman Pipefitter/Plumber seeks position where varied skills can be applied.

EXPERIENCE SUMMARY

Inspect, repair, adjust, install and maintain all piping and associated equipment in a major production plant. Ability to trouble-shoot and repair problems with hydraulic and pneumatic production machinery. Experience with high pressure steam, air, gas, water, acids, chemicals and sewer and waste treatment procedures.

Working experience on steel butt-weld pipe, stainless steel, cast iron, saran, P.V.C., copper, black iron screwed and sprinkler systems for fire control. Maintenance and repair of all plumbing systems, steam heating and hot water heat both industrially and commercially.

Practical knowledge of all power tools, pipe threading machines, hand tools, measuring devices, burning and soldering equipment associated with the pipefitting and plumbing trade.Expertise in the removal of asbestos on piping and other areas (hold Michigan State permit).

EMPLOYMENT HISTORY

Pipefitter/Hydraulic
Fisher Guide Division of General Motors, Flint, MI (1/90 - present)
Residential Plumber
Plumber's and Pipefitters Union #12, Escanaba, MI (2/88-1/90)
Journeyman Pipefitter/Plumber
USX Corporation, Flint, MI (9/86-2/88)
Residential Plumber, Ace Home Heating, Detroit, MI (4/83-9/86)

EDUCATIONAL BACKGROUND

Apprenticeship, Pipefitter/Plumber - USX Corporation
Four-year program - Journeyman, Certification
HVAC Certification Program - Metropolitan Community College

Note: Roy clearly describes his skills in the "Experience Summary" and straight-forwardly shows how and where he acquired those skills.

CONSTANCE BARCLAY

55 Fredonia Lane
Towanda, KS 67144
316-343-2850 (Office)
316-908-2566 (Pager)
316-463-3478 (Home)

SUMMARY

Experienced attorney, member of the Bar in Kansas and Texas, with extensive work in litigation: discovery, depositions, motions, proof hearings, trials, and legal research. Skilled in matrimonial and family law, as well as commercial litigation.

EDUCATION

University of Texas at Austin
J.D., 1983, with distinction
Honors: Law Review,
Moot Court Competition

Baylor University
B.S., Psychology, 1980
Honors: Phi Beta Kappa

EXPERIENCE

Associate, Kramer and Heldref, Wichita, KS
Staff attorney in general law practice. Responsible for all aspects of practice.
Trial experience in Municipal Court, Superior Court, Federal Court, and Common Pleas Court.
Specialize in commercial litigation, often involving extensive research.
Involved in actions worth more than $20 million since joining firm.

Staff Attorney, Holden and Calder, Dallas, Texas
High-volume, metropolitan law firm, with broad general practice.
Litigation involved personal injury and commercial cases.
Handled wide range of legal activities, from real estate to wills and trusts.

Staff Attorney, Legal Aid Society, Fort Worth, TX
Provided legal representation to all clients who met low-income guidelines.
Extensive courtroom experience.
Legal work in child custody, criminal law, motor vehicle, and many other areas.

PERSONAL

Volunteer Attorney, Legal Aid Society of Wichita
Near fluency in spoken Spanish

Note: Constance emphasizes her experience. She lists her education first because it is so impressive. Notice her clear summary of her experience.

LOUIS DeMILLE, Jr.
223 Emerson Rd.
Tucker, GA 30084
(404) 753-8420

CAREER SUMMARY

Over ten years progressive credit analysis and collection experience dealing with commercial, individual and government accounts.

EXPERIENCE

Major Accounts Analyst
GENERAL MANUFACTURING, INC., Atlanta, GA
Total responsibility for the credit maintenance and collection of 40 + major accounts of minimum $1,000,000 net sales, including addressing problems, keeping invoices in good condition and ensuring that accounts stay within credit limits.
  Reduced over-90-day receivables by more than 50%
  Lowered account maintenance paper work by 70%
  Improved "skipped invoice" process, increasing receivables
  Maintained rapport with sales force achieving satisfactory problem resolutions

Credit and Collections Administrator
GATEWAY, INC., Augusta, GA
Total responsibility for credit and collections for entire accounts receivable, including making credit decisions, commission due reports and journal entries for write-offs and adjustments.
  Implemented use of Dun & Bradstreet and NACM credit decision process
  Reduced over-90-day receivables by more than 20%
  Utilized negotiation and communication skills to develop payment schedules and improve
    long-term business relationships with problem accounts

Junior Accountant/Credit & Collection
COMPUTER ASSOCIATES, Tucker, GA
Primary functions involved handling credit and collection of private sector, military and government software lease, lease/purchase and maintenance contracts.
  Conducted contract reviews assuring that commitments were within authorized limits
  Communicated with sales force to evaluate and resolve problem accounts

EDUCATION

DeKalb County College, Decatur, GA
Associates Degree in Applied Science with Major in Business

SKILLS

Working knowledge of IBM PC/Compatible hardware and software;
VAX 11-780; Altos Computer; WordPerfect; MS-Word

Note: Louis has not been continuously employed, so he avoids dates altogether. This puts the focus on what he has done and not when he did it.

RICHARD LING

2888 Lincoln Rd.
Berwyn, IL 60402
(312) 818-4646 Office
(312) 799-3426 Pager

SUMMARY Experienced plant manager with recognized expertise in management of medical centers. Effective supervisor with a commitment to excellence.

EXPERIENCE
Director of Plant Operations, St. Thomas Medical Center, Oak Park, IL (1987-1995)

Responsibilities and Accomplishments
Responsible for $6 million annual budget

Supervise 35 maintenance, power plant and biomedical engineering personnel, through an Assistant Director of Plant Operations and four supervisors

Established an in-house biomedical engineering department, saving over $40,000/year

Obtained a federal grant to partially finance a new Energy Management System, resulting in savings of approximately $150,000 per year

Installed a new incinerator with heat recovery, saving the hospital over $1 million per year

Initiated and coordinated a 12-week training program for all new maintenance personnel

Acted as the owner's representative in all phases of construction of a $45 million addition, bringing the construction to completion on schedule

Note: Medical Center merged with St. Peter's Hospital January 1, 1996

Director of Engineering and Maintenance, Dekalb Community Hospital (1982-1987)
Maintenance Supervisor, Cook County Hospital (1979-1982)
Director of Engineering, Quincey Rehabilitation Center (1975-1979)

EDUCATION
Graduate of Cook County Vocational Technical School
Major: Power Plant Engineering

Maintained continuing education through numerous seminars on all phases of engineering, management, design and construction, and codes and standards given by the Joint Commission on Accreditation of Healthcare Organizations, the American Society for Hospital Engineering, and other state, federal and private educational agencies.

PROFESSIONAL SOCIETIES & AFFILIATIONS
President & Trustee, Executive Hospital Engineers of Illinois
Trustee, National Power Engineers
Vice Chairman, Engineering Advisory Board of Illinois Hospital Association
Member, American Society for Hospital Engineering
Member, National Fire Protection Association

Note: Rich emphasizes his most recent job and then implies the reason it has ended.

INDEX TO SAMPLE RESUMES